Praise for *Keynes's Way to Wealth*

"As I read John Wasik's manuscript, I quickly realized that I had discovered a true gem—fascinating, carefully researched, and (as one would expect from a skilled journalist) snappy and eminently readable. I commend it to you."

—John C. Bogle, founder, The Vanguard Group;
author, *The Clash of the Cultures:
Investment vs. Speculation* (from the Foreword)

"Intelligent investing ultimately depends on having an intelligent theory of the economy. This story of Keynes's life as an investor illustrates this beautifully."

—Robert Shiller, professor of economics, Yale University;
columnist, *The New York Times*;
author, *Finance and the Good Society*

"The great economist John Maynard Keynes speculated and lost bigtime. Out of the ashes, he evolved some great long-term investment strategies that will work for every prudent investor. While picking up tips, you'll also find that this book is a great read."

—Jane Bryant Quinn, author,
Making the Most of Your Money NOW

"I'd always heard Keynes was a talented investor but never knew any of the details. John Wasik's excellent book uncovers that story and reveals Keynes's considerable investing skills. If you enjoy studying great investors, add this book to your list."

—Joe Mansueto, founder and CEO, Morningstar, Inc.

"With the possible exception of Mark Twain, no one surpasses John Maynard Keynes as a source of pithy financial wisdom and sayings. John Wasik's marvelous *Keynes's Way to Wealth* mines the reasoning and investment experiences behind his quotability, a bounty that will simultaneously edify, entertain, and augment your bottom line."

—William J. Bernstein, author, *Masters of the Word: How Media Shaped History*; principal, Efficient Frontier Advisors

"John Wasik's book explodes the myth that John Keynes was a one-trick pony simply espousing government intervention in the economic system. It examines Keynes's little-known role as money manager during volatile times, with his stock-value, opposing-risk, and behavioral concepts providing a successful strategy that has merit for today's investors."

—Andrew Leckey, President, Reynolds National Center for Business Journalism/Reynolds Endowed Chair in Business Journalism, Arizona State University

"Wasik has done a wonderful job showing how Keynes made the transition from trader to a buy-and-hold value investor—who would have made Graham, Dodd, Buffett, and John Bogle proud—and shows you the path to follow in his footsteps."

—Larry Swedroe, principal and the director of research for the BAM Alliance; author, *Think, Act, and Invest Like Warren Buffett*

"John Wasik does a fantastic job of linking economist John Maynard Keynes's economic thoughts to the decisions he made handling wealth on a day-to-day basis. In simple and easy-to-understand language, *Keynes's Way to Wealth* elucidates how Keynes thought about money in the most real way of all and offers valuable incites into his evolution as a writer, economist, and investor."

—Helaine Olen, author, *Pound Foolish: Exposing the Dark Side of the Personal Finance Industry*

"Richard Nixon once said that we are all Keynesians now. But when it comes to our personal investing, only people like Warren Buffett are. Read this wonderful book by John Wasik explaining how Keynes made and protected his own fortune. If we follow the Keynesian investing program set out in this book, we are far more likely to secure the economic future of our grandchildren."

—Thomas Geoghegan, attorney; author, *Only One Thing Can Save Us: Why Our Country Needs to Snap Out of It and Have a New Kind of Labor Movement*

"John Wasik has written a fascinating account of Keynes as an expert investor in commodities, stocks, and bonds. I recommend it to anyone with an interest in Keynes or in investing."

—Zvi Bodie, professor of management, Boston University; coauthor, *Risk Less and Prosper More*

"John's book is a must-read. It provides timeless investment principles through a profile of one of the most fascinating economists in world history. The book provides lessons and advice every investor must know and pragmatic, time-tested ways to build and—almost as importantly—maintain wealth. It's a must-read for every novice as well as highly seasoned investor."

—Andrew Stoltmann, Chicago attorney and investor advocate

"*Keynes's Way to Wealth* does for economics what *The Intelligent Investor* did for picking stocks. Wasik allows us to stand on the shoulders of the most important financial thinkers of the last 100 years. Then he goes one step beyond. You learn the story of the man himself. What were his mistakes and successes that sparked great thoughts? Wasik breathes new life into the most important figure in finance, ever. Keynes was more than an economic thinker—he was a man that that experienced firsthand the agony and ecstasy of financial markets."

—Lee Munson CFA, CFP*, Chief Investment Officer, Portfolio, LLC

"John Wasik does it again! *Keynes's Ways to Wealth* gives new insights into how the world's most famous economist invested. It was revealing to discover that he was not only an innovative money manager, but one who became wealthy guiding several portfolios using what would become value-based principles later used by Warren Buffett and others."

—Tom Lydon, publisher, *ETF Trends*

"John Wasik surprises us with the story of a money manager and unexpected capitalist: John Maynard Keynes."

"Economist John Maynard Keynes, who died in 1946, remains a political lightning rod on the left and right. Wasik reveals a Keynes we don't know. He was a man who through trial and error and, as Wasik says, "a lot of gumption" devised a sensible strategy for all investors, whether they watch Fox or MSNBC."

"The author of this book sets out to fill a gap in the vast literature on Keynes, namely his investment philosophy analyzed in the context of his life, work, and legacy. It is a creditable endeavor, offering a very readable account that will doubtless appeal to the nonspecialist, but also to scholars who may not be as knowledgeable about Keynes's investments as the author of this book."

"In his latest book, *Keynes's Ways to Wealth*, John Wasik pens an exceptionally well-researched and compelling treatise of an often overlooked aspect of John Maynard Keynes—that he was a risk-averse speculator who bet his own, and other people's money, on commodities, currencies, stocks, and bonds during a time that preceded the existence of traditional institutional hedge fund or money managers. In this fascinating account, and without wading into weighty economic discourse best left to theoreticians, Wasik shows how Keynes's role as a successful value-investor capitalist during war and the Depression, as much as or perhaps more so than his academic background, provided the foundation upon which his economic theories and financial practices were formulated."

KEYNES'S
WAY *to*
WEALTH

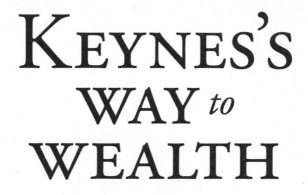

KEYNES'S WAY *to* WEALTH

Timeless
Investment Lessons
=== *from the* ===
Great Economist

JOHN F. WASIK

New York   Chicago   San Francisco   Athens   London   Madrid
Mexico City   Milan   New Delhi   Singapore   Sydney   Toronto

1 2 3 4 5 6 7 8 9 0   DOC/DOC   1 9 8 7 6 5 4 3

ISBN   978-0-07-181547-5
MHID   0-07-181547-3

e-ISBN   978-0-07-181548-2
e-MHID   0-07-181548-1

This publication is designed to provide accurate and authoritative information in regard to the subject matter covered. It is sold with the understanding that neither the author nor the publisher is engaged in rendering legal, accounting, securities trading, or other professional services. If legal advice or other expert assistance is required, the services of a competent professional person should be sought.

—From a Declaration of Principles Jointly Adopted by a Committee of the American Bar Association and a Committee of Publishers and Associations

Library of Congress Cataloging-in-Publication Data
Wasik, John F.
  Keynes's way to wealth : timeless investment lessons from the great economist / John F. Wasik.
     pages cm
  ISBN-13: 978-0-07-181547-5 (hardback)
  ISBN-10: 0-07-181547-3 (hardback)
1. Portfolio management. 2. Investment analysis. 3. Investments. 4. Keynes, John Maynard, 1883–1946. I. Title.
  HG4529.5.W374   2013
  332.6–dc23

                                                                              2013020008

To Arthur Stanley Wasik

Contents

Foreword: Keynes the Investor   ix

Preface   xxi

Acknowledgments   xxv

Introduction   xxvii

1   Birth of a Speculator   1

2   Economic Consequences   15

3   Macro Versus Micro: The New Treatise on Money   35

4   Building Portfolios with Opposed Risks   53

5   The Birth of Value   71

6   Animal Spirits: The Birth of Behavioral Investing   87

7   Keynes's Pets   105

8   Keynes's Heirs   123

9   Keynes's Keys to Wealth   137

Epilogue: The Once and Future Keynes   151

A   Visiting Keynes Country and His Other Sources of Wealth   157

B   The Independent Investment Company Portfolio   161

Endnotes   169

Bibliographical Notes   183

Index   189

Foreword

Keynes the Investor

IN THIS TURBULENT ECONOMIC ENVIRONMENT OF OUR "POST-bubble" age, worldwide focus is on two substantially opposite government policies in dealing with the global slowdown. One is based on the free market concepts advocated by the Austrian economist Friedrich Hayek (1899–1992)—cutting government expenditures, reducing deficits and debt levels, and letting a nation's economy respond with growth through unfettered markets for goods and services.

"Keynesian economics," on the other hand, as advocated by the British economist John Maynard Keynes (1883–1946), calls for strong government intervention, with the goal of increasing aggregate economic demand by so-called "pump priming"—raising government expenditures and increasing deficits and debt (at least until economic growth resumes), with federal stimulus compensating for the lack of private spending.

When, as an Economics major at Princeton University in 1950, I first read Keynes's magnum opus on this subject, *The General Theory of Employment, Interest and Money* (1936), I confess that

I found the book's message a tad over my young head. But one chapter, Chapter XII, on "The State of Long-Term Expectation," was both clear and persuasive to me. That chapter, laced with investment wisdom, made a major impact on my 1951 senior thesis, "The Economic Role of the Investment Company." What's more, Keynes's wisdom has also found its way into many of the essays and lectures I've subsequently delivered, as well as 9 of the 10 books that I've written since 1993. Keynes the *investor* then, not Keynes the *economist*, has been the inspiration for my central investment philosophy.

So it was with particular delight that I learned that journalist John F. Wasik would focus on that very issue—Keynes's investment wisdom—in the book you are now holding, *Keynes's Way to Wealth*. As I read John Wasik's manuscript, I quickly realized that I had discovered a true gem—fascinating, carefully researched, and (as one would expect from a skilled journalist) snappy and eminently readable. I commend it to you.

As the author's subtitle—*Timeless Investment Lessons from the Great Economist*—suggests, Keynes's career as a brilliant investor provides today's investor with a sound foundation for developing and implementing an intelligent investment strategy. In his Chapter 10, Wasik gives us 10 rules—"Keys to Wealth"—which I fully endorse. Indeed, they form the central principles for my own investment portfolio. Even more important, those keys to successful investing largely constitute the foundational investment strategies that I inculcated at The Vanguard Group of Investment Companies, which I founded in 1974. These fundamental values, in fact, were in many respects built on the ideas I expressed in that Princeton thesis more than six decades ago. They have met the test of time.

The role that Lord Keynes played in my long career provides an extraordinary example of how sound ideas, essentially simple to understand and easy to describe, can echo over the years. Keynes, I think, would marvel about their durability in the investment thinking—and investment programs—of investors nearly 80 years after *General Theory* and its eye-opening Chapter XII were published.

Let me begin the story when Keynes made his critical distinction between investment and speculation. In 1925, he took on the foolish predilection of investors to implicitly assume that the future will resemble the past. Keynes warned: "It is dangerous to apply to the future inductive arguments based on past experience unless we can distinguish the broad reasons for what it [the past] was."[1]

Enterprise and Speculation

A decade later, in *General Theory*, he focused on the two broad reasons that explain the returns on stocks. The first was what he called *enterprise*—"forecasting the prospective yield of an asset over its entire life." The second was *speculation*—"forecasting the psychology of the market." Together, these two factors explain "The State of Long-Term Expectation" for investors.

From his vantage point in London, Keynes observed that "in one of the greatest investment markets in the world, namely, New York, the influence of speculation is enormous. . . . It is rare for an American to 'invest for income,' and he will not readily purchase an investment except in the hope of capital appreciation. This is only another way of saying that he is attaching his hopes to a favorable change in the conventional basis of valuation, i.e., that he is a speculator." Today, almost eight decades after Keynes wrote those words, the same situation prevails, only far more strongly.

Lord Keynes's confidence that short-term speculation would overwhelm long-term enterprise was based on the then-dominant ownership of stock by individuals, largely ignorant of business operations or valuations, leading to excessive, even absurd short-term market fluctuations driven by events of an ephemeral and insignificant character. Short-term fluctuations in the earnings of existing investments, he argued (correctly), would lead to unreasoning waves of optimistic and pessimistic sentiment.

While competition between expert professionals, possessing judgment and knowledge beyond that of the average private investor, Keynes added, should correct the vagaries caused by ignorant individuals, the energies and skill of the professional investor would come to be largely concerned, not with making superior long-term forecasts of the probable yield of an investment over its whole life, but with foreseeing changes in the conventional basis of valuation a short time ahead of the general public. He therefore described the market as "a battle of wits to anticipate the basis of conventional valuation a few months hence, rather than the prospective yield of an investment over a long term of years."

A Young Student Disagrees with an Old Master

I cited Keynes's conclusions in my 1951 senior thesis, but the young student had the temerity to disagree with the old master. Rather than professional investors succumbing to the speculative psychology of ignorant market participants, I argued, these professional investors would focus on enterprise. In what I predicted—accurately—would become a far larger mutual fund industry, our portfolio managers would "supply the market with a demand for securities that is *steady, sophisticated, enlightened, and analytic* [italics added], a demand that is based essentially on the [intrinsic] performance of the corporation rather than the public appraisal reflected in the price of its shares." Alas, the sophisticated and analytic focus on enterprise that I had predicted from the industry's expert professional investors has utterly failed to materialize. Rather, the emphasis on speculation by mutual funds has actually increased manifold. Call the score, Keynes 1, Bogle 0.

Interestingly, Keynes was well aware of the fallibility of forecasting stock returns, noting that "it would be foolish in forming our expectations to attach great weight to matters which are very uncertain." He added that "by very uncertain I do not mean the same thing as 'improbable.'" Keynes, therefore, made no attempt to quantify the relationship between enterprise and speculation in shaping the returns on individual stocks; he also didn't consider the idea of diversifying away individual stock risks by owning a diversified portfolio of hundreds of stocks. Decades later, however, it occurred to me to focus on stock *portfolios* and quantify those relationships.

Putting Numbers on Keynes's Distinction

By the late 1980s, based on my research on the financial markets and my own firsthand experience, I had concluded that the two essential sources of equity returns were: (1) *economics,* and (2) *emotions.* What Keynes had described as enterprise I called "economics." What Keynes termed "speculation," I found well defined by "emotions." I defined enterprise as *investment return*—the initial dividend yield on a portfolio of stocks plus the subsequent annual rate of earnings growth. I defined emotions as *speculative return*—the change in the price that investors are willing to pay for each dollar of earnings—essentially, the return that is generated by changes in the valuation (the discount rate) that investors place on future earnings of the corporations in the portfolio.

Simply adding speculative return to investment return produces the *total* return generated by the stock market portfolios. For example, if stocks begin a decade with a dividend yield of 4 percent and experience subsequent earnings growth of 5 percent, the *investment* return would be 9 percent. If the price-earnings ratio rises from 15 times to 20 times, that 33 percent increase, spread over a decade, would translate into an additional *speculative* return of about 3 percentage points annually. Simply adding the two returns together, the total return on stocks would come to 12 percent. It's not very complicated!

This remarkably simple numeric approach of separating enterprise and speculation (i.e., investment return and speculative return) has been borne out in practice. Indeed I have the temerity (again!) to suggest that Lord Keynes would respect this mathematical extension of his concept. Decade after decade over the past century, using the 500 stocks in the Standard and Poor's Stock Index as our portfolio, we can account, with remarkable precision, for the total returns actually earned by U.S. stocks (Table F-1).

The *investment return* on stocks (Column 3) has proven to be remarkably susceptible to reasonable expectations. The initial dividend yield (Column 1), a crucial—but underrated—factor in shaping stock returns—is known at the moment one invests. The steady contribution of dividend yields to investment return during each decade has always been a positive, only once outside the range of 3 percent to 5 percent annually.

With the exception of the depression-ridden 1930s, the contribution of earnings growth (Column 2) was also positive in every decade, usually running between 4 percent and 7 percent per year. Only twice were total investment returns (during the 1930s and the 2000s) less than 6 percent annually, and only twice more than 12 percent. But if we recognize that corporate earnings have, with remarkable consistency, grown at about the rate of the U.S. Gross Domestic Product (GDP), this relative consistency is hardly surprising.

Speculative return is, well, speculative, and has alternated from positive to negative over the decades. If P/E ratios are historically

TABLE F-1 The Sources of Returns on a Diversified Stock Portfolio*

	1		2		3		4		5
			Investment Return						
	Dividend Yield	+	**Earnings Growth**	=	**(1+2) Total**	+	**Speculative Return****	=	**(3+4) Total Market Return**
1900s	3.5%		4.7%		8.2%		0.8%		9.0%
1910s	4.3		2.0		6.3		-3.4		2.9
1920s	5.9		5.6		11.5		3.3		14.8
1930s	4.5		-5.6		-1.1		0.3		-0.8
1940s	5.0		9.9		14.9		-6.3		8.6
1950s	6.9		3.9		10.8		9.3		20.1
1960s	3.1		5.5		8.6		-1.0		7.6
1970s	3.5		9.9		13.4		-7.5		5.9
1980s	5.2		4.4		9.6		7.7		17.3
1990s	3.2		7.4		10.6		7.2		17.8
2000s	1.2		0.8		2.0		-3.2		-1.2
1900–2009 Average	4.5%	+	4.3%	=	8.8%	+	0.3%	=	9.1%

*Standard & Poor's 500 Stock Index.

**Change in valuation, measured by decade-long annual rate of increase or decrease in price/earnings multiple.

low (say, below 10 times), they have been likely to rise over the subsequent decade. If they are historically high (say, above 20 times), they have been likely to decline (though in neither case do we know *when* the change is coming). Nonetheless, as Keynes aptly reminded us, certainty about the future never exists, nor are probabilities always borne out. But this simple method of calculating investment return and speculative return and then combining them to project the total return on stocks has been a successful way to establish reasonable expectations for stock market returns over the decades.

The point is this: Over the very long run, it is the *economics* if investing—enterprise—that has determined total return; the evanescent *emotions* of investing—speculation—so important over the short run, have ultimately proven to be virtually meaningless. As shown in Table F-1, over the past 110 years, the 9.1 percent average annual return on U.S. stocks has been composed of 8.8 percentage points of investment return (an average dividend yield of 4.5 percent plus average annual earnings growth of 4.3 percent), and only 0.3 percent of speculative return, born of an inevitably period-dependent increase in the price-earnings ratio from 10 times to 18 times, amortized over the full period. In sum, investing in American business for the long term has been a winner's game.

"Animal Spirits"

Keynes closed his Chapter XII with some thoughts about the instability of speculation. In so doing, he gave us a phrase that belongs to the ages—"animal spirits."

> Even apart from the instability due to speculation, there is the instability due to the characteristic of human nature that a

large proportion of our positive activities depend on spontaneous optimism rather than on a mathematical expectation
whether moral or hedonistic or economic. Most, probably, of
our decisions to do something positive, the full consequences
of which will be drawn out over many days to come, can only
be taken as a result of animal spirits—of a spontaneous urge
to action rather than inaction, and not as the outcome of a
weighted average of quantitative benefits multiplied by quantitative probabilities.

Enterprise only pretends to itself to be mainly actuated by
the statements in its own prospectus, however candid and sin-
cere. Only a little more than an expedition to the South Pole,
is it based on an exact calculation of benefits to come. Thus if
the animal spirits are dimmed and the spontaneous optimism
falters, leaving us to depend on nothing but a mathematical
expectation, enterprise will fade and die . . .

In his comments that conclude Chapter XII, Keynes seems to
endorse my humble attempts to quantify his conclusions about
how the stock market works. When he urges investors not to conclude "that everything depends on waves of irrational psychology,"
he reaffirms the coming and going of speculative return. And
when he describes the state of long-term expectations as "often
being steady," he is noting, really, that it is investment return—
economics rather than emotions—that calls the tune of investing
over a lifetime.

Of course Keynes was right when he emphasized that investment decisions affecting the future cannot depend on a strict
mathematical expectation. The future is always uncertain. But
were Keynes with us today, he would likely marvel at the way
that diversification can reduce the risk of individual stocks and
narrow forecasts, and—as far as we can tell—enhance our ability

to predict that the earnings of the companies in a portfolio of all stocks (in the U.S. at least, and perhaps the entire global portfolio) should grow at a rate that parallels the long-term growth of the economy of the nation, and of the world.

A Major Contribution to Keynes's Legacy

Remarkably, given the vast changes in the financial landscape since Keynes's magnum opus was published nearly eight decades ago, the relevance of his ideas continues to resonate today. Most compelling, perhaps, is the large group of practiced, experienced, and respected investors whose strategies echo those of John Maynard Keynes. *Keynes's Way to Wealth* cites, among others, Warren E. Buffett, Berkshire-Hathaway's Oracle of Omaha; Benjamin Graham, author of the classic *The Intelligent Investor*; David Swensen, pioneering investment manager of Yale University's thriving endowment fund; and Jeremy Grantham, the articulate (and rarely wrong) manager at GMO.

Of course I'm honored to be included in John Wasik's pantheon, largely for my 1975 creation of the world's first index mutual fund, only months after the creation of Vanguard. With its unique mutual (shareholder-owned) structure, Vanguard is now the largest fund firm in the world. Among all of these long-term investors, I may well owe Keynes the most. For his wisdom on the sources of stock market returns—enterprise and speculation—has played a defining role in the way that I've tried to help investors accumulate wealth.

Keynes's Way to Wealth is a major addition to the numerous books, essays, and studies of the life and work of John Maynard Keynes. His relevance to the investment world of today is also reflected in John Wasik's listing of "Ten Keys to Wealth." Here, the author concludes by describing the way that Lord Keynes expressed his philosophy of life: it is those "who can keep alive, and cultivate into a fuller perfection, the art of life itself, and do not sell themselves for the means of life, who will be able to enjoy the abundance when it comes." Despite today's widespread materialism—especially in America's financial sector—John Wasik urges a similar philosophy for the investor challenged by today's fragile world economy. "Put your investing on autopilot with a sound plan that meets your goals and monitor it once a year. Then go out and live."

John C. Bogle
Valley Forge, PA
July 15, 2013

Preface

OVER THE PAST 80 YEARS, THE GLOBAL ECONOMIC SYSTEM HAS been indelibly influenced by the groundbreaking work of John Maynard Keynes. Yet few people know what a successful investor Keynes was. In fact, he was one of the greatest investors of the twentieth century, given that the period in which he was investing in spanned two world wars and the Great Depression. Not only did his economic theory strive to save capitalism from itself, but his own investment prowess proved how much he believed in the power of markets. There was no more fervent believer in—and preserver of—capitalism than Keynes. Unlike most great economists, Keynes's worldview was guided by his investments and profited from them. Since he was a trader and money manager for more than two decades, he knew and understood markets better than most academic economists. His investment strategies not only made him rich, but enriched three other institutions.

Unfortunately, Keynes has become the St. Sebastian for free-market advocates and zealots who mistakenly believe that he was out to destroy democracy and capitalism and to enshrine government as the final arbiter of economic behavior. Nothing could be further from the truth. Keynes was a true believer in capitalism, and his rousing success as an investor shows the degree to which he embraced markets nearly all his life.

Among other things, Keynes genuinely enjoyed being a speculator and an investor. He called his favorite stocks his "pets." In addition to thinking through the ideas that would rescue the Western economies (and Japan and eventually China) after two devastating cataclysms, he managed money for his own portfolio, his friends, and several institutions. Keynes was one of the first hedge fund managers, and he established some time-honored principles that the best investors follow today. Without Keynes, the "value" and "behavioral" schools of investors that have given us Warren Buffett, Jeremy Grantham, and George Soros would not have been the same.

Upon digging into Keynes's lecture notes from more than 100 years ago, I discovered something even more revealing about Keynes. Not only did he have a brilliant understanding of markets, but he became more insightful as he aged. His investment activity informed his economic theory. Like many of us, he made numerous mistakes speculating, but he managed to learn from his experience and conclude that he was looking at the wrong things. He completely changed his mind, revised the way he was investing, and compounded his wealth after losing two fortunes. Unlike most people's, his intellectual growth was *enhanced* by his blunders. Remarkably, he still was able to make money in some of the worst markets in history.

I can relate to Keynes's life as an investor because I've traveled a similar path as an investor and as a journalist and author writing about money. During my early days, I speculated in commodities and eventually concluded that I couldn't possibly anticipate market movements with the limited information I had. At best, I was guessing. Then I picked stocks that I liked, only to see them tank during several crashes. Finally I realized that I couldn't beat what Keynes called the "animal spirits" of the market. I stopped trying to time the market and followed the advice of Warren Buffett and

John Bogle, founder of the Vanguard Group. I mostly stayed put in index funds, which hold baskets of stocks and bonds.

What I'm hoping you'll discover from this book is that Keynes's ideas, insights and portfolio moves not only are relevant today, but are pragmatic, time-tested ways to build wealth. They demonstrate how he learned *not* to try to outguess the markets. If he were alive today, Keynes would tell us to stop fighting the riptide of market prognosticators, stock pickers, business headlines, and blowhards on business channels.

In this book, I will show you how his thinking as an investor evolved, and how he shaped the world around him and our ever-complex economic environment. Most important, I'll illustrate how to apply what he learned and provide some focus on how contemporary investors still use his insights. In the end, you can not only develop a prudent, risk-appropriate investment plan, but create a life plan for prosperity, one that harnesses the energy of the market's animal spirits instead of being spooked by it.

John F. Wasik
2013

Acknowledgments

I'D LIKE TO THANK A NUMBER OF PEOPLE WHO HELPED ME, either directly or indirectly: Theresa Amato, Zvi Bodie, Debbie Bosanek (a spokesperson for Warren Buffett), David Chambers, Elroy Dimson, Thomas Geoghegan, Dick Longworth, Carol Loomis, Jan Toporowsky, Victoria Chick, and Geoffrey Harcourt. Romesh Vaitilingam of the Royal Economic Society helped me connect with several Keynesians.

Patricia McGuire, Peter Jones, and Peter Monteith at the Cambridge University Archives were particularly diligent in helping me navigate the extensive material on Keynes in the King's College Archives. Susan Antilla, Bill Bernstein, Diana Henriques, Paul Krugman, Joe Mansueto, Lee Munson, Sylvia Nasar, Jane Bryant Quinn, Alice Schroeder, Robert Shiller, Meir Statman, Lee Munson, and Wally Winter also provided invaluable insights and assistance. My agent, Robert Shepard, and my editor, Zachary Gajewski, stood by me when it counted. Vanguard founder Jack Bogle wrote a splendid foreword that stands on its own as a fountain of insights on investing. I am humbled that all of these people chose to help me bring this book into the world.

The reference librarians from my hometown of Grayslake, Illinois, were invaluable in tracking down obscure economics texts and articles. And the archivists at the University of Cambridge were instrumental in finding, retrieving, and copying the documents I needed from Keynes's papers at King's College.

Most of all, I'd like to thank and commend the patience of my loving family: my wife, Kathleen Rose, and my daughters, Sarah Virginia and Julia Theresa.

Introduction

Keynes's intellect was the sharpest and clearest
that I have ever known. When I argued with him,
I felt that I took my life in my hands, and I seldom
emerged without feeling something of a fool.
I was sometimes inclined to feel that so much
cleverness must be incompatible with depth,
but I do not think this feeling was justified.

—BERTRAND RUSSELL[1]

THE FAIRMONT HOTEL BALLROOM IN CHICAGO WAS WHIRRING
with excitement as Nobel Prize winner Paul Krugman walked to
the podium in front of 2,000 people. Speaking to the Chicago
Council on Global Affairs on the frigid last day of January 2013,
Krugman assailed the state of the American economy, which was
slowly recovering, but which he characterized as still being in a
depression. The *New York Times* columnist and Princeton professor weighed in on what it would take to restore full employment, a subject that had haunted John Maynard Keynes for most
of his career. This evening, though, Krugman was a rock star.
The audience had braved subzero windchill to receive his wisdom.
Like many in his profession, he was expounding on how to fix
the American economy, which was still reeling from the recession

that had followed the 2008 meltdown. As 2013 dawned, U.S. unemployment was still hovering around 8 percent, and Congress was wrestling with making more than $1 trillion in budget cuts and raising the debt ceiling to allow more borrowing. As one of the world's foremost Keynesians, Krugman gave prescriptions for what ailed the economy.

Using the framework for describing crisis economics that Keynes developed in his *General Theory of Employment, Interest and Money*, Krugman called the post-2008 period a "lesser depression" because of the severe lack of consumer demand and corporate spending.

The presence of Keynes, as channeled by Krugman (although he never mentioned Keynes by name), was deeply felt in the grand ballroom. What the English economist had first recommended during the Great Depression was being revisited through the often-distorted lens of twentieth-century macroeconomics, which Keynes had fathered during one of the darkest decades of the century. Why was Keynes still a potent influence some three generations after his death? Although the economist had become a lightning rod for often ineffective and overwhelming government intervention, his work came back into vogue following the 2008 meltdown. When faced with a devastating recession that had cratered the housing and credit markets, thrown millions out of work, and nearly crippled the global economy, both Congress and the Federal Reserve adopted Keynesian approaches in an attempt to stimulate the economy. While the results are still mixed, this forced a new look at what the economist was all about and why he is still relevant.

Yet the essence of Keynes goes far beyond his theories and prescriptions, which are still engendering vigorous debate. The economist loved investing and markets. He staked his own money, managed millions for institutions, lost a bundle, but somehow managed to make a fortune in one of the worst times to be an investor. This is the largely unknown story that few economists or biographers have told.

Beginnings

Keynes was born in Cambridge, England, on June 5, 1883, a child born into middle-class privilege during a period when Victorian England was lurching into the modern age. At the time, England's position as the world's largest economic power seemed secure, and its dominion extended from Australia to Canada. Keynes's father, John Neville, was a Cambridge don and administrator. He published texts on economic method and philosophy. His mother, Florence Ada Brown, was the daughter of an esteemed Congregationalist minister who often "took up good causes, but never at the expense of her family," writes Keynes's biographer Robert Skidelsky.[2]

Armed with a formidable intellect, arrogant confidence, and a keen sense of his place in the world, Keynes excelled in his studies at Eton, Britain's top public school, where he obtained a scholarship in 1897. Mathematics was his particular forte, although he was also interested in all the arts. By 1902 he was admitted to Cambridge, again on scholarship. While he admitted that math never pleased him all that much, he gained a first-class degree in the subject in Part I of the Mathematical Tripos (final honors degree exams). Along the way, he developed several enduring friendships, enjoyed a robust social life, and communed with great minds like the philosopher/mathematician Bertrand Russell, ethicist G. E. Moore, and sage economist Alfred Marshall, a mentor who opened Keynes's mind to economics. He was accepted into a secret society called the Apostles, which was the Cambridge equivalent of Skull and Bones at Yale.

It was within the Apostles that Keynes met lifelong friends such as Lytton Strachey, who later moved to London and socialized with luminaries like the author Virginia Woolf in the Bloomsbury circle. Falling in and out of love with various young men—artist Duncan Grant was a lover from 1908 to 1911—Keynes lived a life of passion while embracing the then-stolid art of economics. His inner and outer circles of friends and acquaintances would later include some of the greatest intellects and leaders of the early twentieth century, from George Bernard Shaw to Winston Churchill. Witty but sometimes insufferable, he could entrance people in conversation at one moment, then rudely dismiss them with sarcasm in a heartbeat. Not even those who despised him, though, believed that he was anything less than brilliant when he sported his extensive knowledge of history, art, philosophy, politics, and math. He was truly an Edwardian da Vinci.

A Moral Science

Keynes and his fellow Cambridge Apostles were enraptured by the ethical philosophy of Moore, whose *Principia Ethica*, published in 1903, became their secular bible. Like every ethicist before him, Moore asked the difficult questions: What is good? How can we know what is good? What is a good life? Keynes would later weave Moore's philosophy into his vision of economics in a broader attempt to create a better world, one without war, strife, unemployment, and poverty. Inspired by Moore, Keynes rejected eighteenth-century utilitarian philosopher Jeremy Bentham's "hedonic calculus," which attempted to quantify various types of pleasure mathematically. Along with his Bloomsbury friends, Keynes abandoned strict religious ideas of right and wrong and pursued beauty, pleasure, and artistic pursuits:

The appropriate subjects of a passionate contemplation and communion were a beloved person, beauty and truth, and one's prime objects in life were love, the creation and enjoyment of aesthetic experience and the pursuit of knowledge.[3]

Keynes called his rebellious ethos that of an *immoralist*; he did not see himself as amoral, since he believed that he was a Utopian, but he was someone "who believes in a continuing moral progress." It was an antifundamentalist view of the world that "repudiated all versions of original sin."[4] The corset-bound world of Victorian morality essentially ended with Keynes's group and his outer circle, which included D. H. Lawrence, the author of the ribald *Lady Chatterley's Lover*, which Keynes endorsed. Under the influence of Moore, Russell, and other radical thinkers, Keynes was guided by "rational self-interest," which also happens to be a bedrock of most classical views on economic behavior. Marshall was his tutor in economics.

As one who thought and loved freely and indulged passionately in the arts, Keynes was able to break the mold of classical economics and the way we view markets and mass behavior. Although he was schooled in the idea that economics was a moral science, he also introduced a sense of fairness and justice into economics. He was genuinely concerned about those who had been thrown out of work during the Depression, and he abhorred the twin evils of inflation and deflation. His British sense of fair play set him to work on making markets and economies more stable.

In keeping with what a young man of his station was expected to do once he obtained his degree, Keynes took the national civil service exam in 1906 and placed second. That enabled him to work as a clerk in the India Office, which fed his interest in macroeconomics, the superstructure that supported the flow of money throughout the civilized world. After two years, though, he was restless and yearned for greater challenges. He lectured at Cambridge until the outbreak of World War I. He was 31 at the time and held a post in the Treasury from 1915 until 1919. After the war, his literary and economic career thrust him onto the world stage, and his ideas on macroeconomics became his calling card.

The Jazz-Age Economist

Keynes was a jazz-age genius before anyone had heard of Louis Armstrong. As he probed the finances of India and the atonal, harsh language of the Versailles Treaty, he discovered in economics a calling that spoke to him. In the wake of the Great War, he was suddenly a player who was strutting and fretting upon the world stage—an improviser who was singing a new melody. And nearly everyone who mattered—except the principals who were negotiating the reparations from Germany—was listening to him. His *Economic Consequences of the Peace*, which condemned the victors of World War I and showed how and why Germany would ultimately turn to fascism, made him a superstar. The book was a bestseller and made him a must-read on both sides of the Atlantic, cementing his place in the spotlight. Keynes was the insider who gave a raspberry to the elites who were running governments and sowing the economic seeds for another war. But when he spoke, it was to make a difference. The "war to end all wars" was doomed to be repeated. Keynes told us what would go wrong as a result of the Versailles Treaty—and that treaty eventually produced Hitler and the most horrific conflict in human history. Although he annoyed, chided, and berated the Euro-American power class, they couldn't ignore him, and they asked for his counsel repeatedly from 1919 until 1946, when he died.

Keynes's place in history, though often bitterly contested, is such that he deserves a seat next to Churchill, Einstein, and Franklin Delano Roosevelt. Both Churchill and Roosevelt listened to his advice, although they didn't always take it. Not only did Keynes help finance World War II for Britain, but he laid out the solid architecture of Keynesian economics, which posits that government can make a huge difference in creating demand during economic downturns. While the historical Keynes rarely evokes a weak response—he's seen as either a devil or a saint—the influence he has had in terms of creating prosperity and averting war over economic issues is undeniable. The Bretton Woods Accords, which set up the World Bank and the International Monetary Fund, were Keynes's children. There is no Western government that hasn't employed Keynesian remedies over the past 60 years. Some are still doing so; others refuse to do so. As Krugman notes in a splendid introduction to Keynes's *General Theory of Employment, Interest and Money*:

> A businessman who warns that confidence poses risks for the economy is a Keynesian, whether he knows it or not. A politician who promises that his tax cuts will create jobs by putting spending money in people's pockets is a Keynesian, even if he comes to abhor the doctrine. Even self-proclaimed supply-side economists, who claim to have refuted Keynes, fall back on unmistakably Keynesian stories to explain why the economy turned down in a given year.[5]

How does Keynesian economics inform us today? It may be an antidote to lasting recessions, although his approach has been so politicized and bowdlerized that it's hard to see it in practice. While this book won't be examining that question in any depth, I will endeavor to show how it can be a lens for modern investors.

As the late investor Barton Biggs observed in his charming book *Hedgehogging*, "Every serious investor needs to understand the Keynesian model, for it is an integral part of the way the world works."[6]

Keynes the Investor

Whatever position you take on Keynesian economics, a little-known part of his life is that he was a stunningly active and successful investor. Sometime around the start of World War I, he started speculating in stocks, currencies, and commodities. Although he had been investing money received from awards and birthday gifts since he was a youth, King's College began to enlist him in the management of its financial affairs in the first decade of the twentieth century, a role that he continued to play until his death in 1946. He later managed money for his friends, his family, and insurance companies at a time when there was so such thing as formal training for institutional money managers. In keeping with his jazzy persona and penetrating intellect, he invented management techniques along the way. He was undoubtedly the godfather of the behavioral school of economics, and he has had profound influence upon the value school. Despite those who accuse Keynes of being a doting protector of government and socialist values, when you look at how he invested, it's clear that he was a die-hard capitalist. During the time when he was an adjunct advisor to the British government, he bought and sold stocks, bonds, currencies, and commodities. His spectacular success showed not only his passion for making money, but his growing aversion to losing it. As someone who had gained two fortunes through his trading prowess and lost them through his hubris, Keynes is a stellar example of how an investor can learn, fall on his face more than once, and still come out ahead.

What I'll share with you is how Keynes achieved his remarkable fortune during a time in which fear, panic, inflation, deflation, mass unemployment, and war took turns devastating the world's largest economies. Not only did Keynes prosper, but he developed some essential ideas that will help you achieve financial well-being. Yet please don't mistake this for a detailed analysis of his theories. I am not an economist, and I don't pretend to understand all the nuances of his ideas. I'll show you what he learned, what worked, what failed, and how modern investors have embraced his ideas.

Perhaps emboldened by his erudite bad boy success and his access to power, Keynes's passions took an interesting turn after World War I. Profits from his books and his teaching income allowed him to live the life of an aristocrat. He invested in art, traveled to the Continent, and picked up Impressionist masterpieces for a song after 1919. With considerable disposable income, he adopted a new hobby: speculation. This led him to place bets on currencies and commodities in the postwar environment. As Europe meandered from the Versailles Treaty to rebuilding, the continent's economy was shaky, but Keynes had a front-row seat to figure out when to go long and when to short. He did so with abandon.

First, however, let's go back to before World War I, when Keynes was getting his feet wet as a fellow at Cambridge, lecturing students on the basics of economics and finance and grasping how the world worked.

KEYNES'S
WAY *to*
WEALTH

1

Birth of a Speculator

Keynes knew how to play the market better than almost anyone else living or dead. He stayed in bed each morning until lunchtime and made not one but two vast fortunes by directing his brokers on exactly what to buy and sell.

—NICHOLAS WAPSHOTT

BEFORE HE EMBARKED UPON THE LIFE OF AN ACADEMIC WHO would later counsel world leaders, the world's most influential economist began a career as a civil servant. Having scored second in a civil service exam in 1906 (he was enraged at his second-place finish) he accepted a post as a junior clerk in the government's India Office in London, where his role was humdrum. Although he didn't have much interest in India, which the British Raj ruled completely at the time, the position gave him key insights into how money worked in society and its importance to the functioning of civilization. It was hardly a glamorous job, though: Keynes's first task in the office was to ship 10 Aylshire bulls to Bombay.[1]

Being in the heart of London gave Keynes access to his Bloomsbury friends, their engaging parties, and trips to the continent, including Spain and the French Pyrenees. As he excelled in divining the vagaries of the British-dominated Indian economy, which later led to a book, his expertise won him important supporters in government. He eventually joined the Royal Commission on Indian Currency and Finance.

Had Keynes remained an obscure government employee, he would probably have been forgotten. But he was bored and began working on a book on probability. He also wanted to return to Cambridge, where he could stimulate his intellect by being a scholar and lecturer. By mid-1908, he was back at King's College. The following year, he started lecturing on money, credit, prices, and the stock market (in 1910).

It's at the end of the twentieth century's first decade that we see Keynes's growing interest in markets, investing, and speculation. In his lecture notes, we see a curious mind that has, up until that point, not been directly engaged in investing, but had a yearning to explore. His lecture on the stock market in the Lenten term of 1910 calls it "essentially a practical subject, which cannot properly be taught by book or lecture." This may have been the point when Keynes briefly left the world of theory and book learning and prepared to engage in a subject that stirred his inner trader. Keynes invited his students into his rooms at King's College, his lanky body relaxed in a commodious armchair. Embracing the tradition of dons meeting with students in an intimate setting, he listened intently as his students presented papers in his Political Economy Club. Ever the Bloomsbury free spirit, he adorned his walls with seminude paintings by his lover Duncan Grant. Not only could students address serious economic issues, but they could gaze upon grape pickers and dancers. It's hard to tell their reactions to the brilliant but aspiring bohemian don, but many of the students later became his friends and collaborators. Keynes was incredibly loyal to them.

Although Keynes bluntly told his students, "I have myself no practical *knowledge* [crossed out] experience of the questions involved," he started his course by encouraging his pupils to read the *Economist* and other financial weeklies. How did Keynes get the investing bug? Perhaps it happened in 1905, when he was studying directly with his mentor, Alfred Marshall, the leading light of late-Victorian economics. When he returned to Cambridge in 1908, he became assistant bursar, which involved handling financial accounts and investments. When I asked Robert Skidelsky, the author of the most comprehensive biography of Keynes, when he first saw evidence of Keynes's serious interest in investing, he surmised that it was before 1910, when "like [George] Soros, I think he used the financial markets to test his theory of probability."[2]

More Than a Hunch

To Keynes, investing must have presented some compelling intellectual challenges. What was the probability of a security going up or down? What were the factors involved? How did price movements obey the laws of averages and chance? What was one to do in the face of uncertainty, when events didn't follow the predictable rules of statistics? Since he was schooled as a mathematician and had produced a work on probability during his early teaching career (*A Treatise on Probability*, which was eventually published in 1921), like any inquiring investor, he wanted to know the odds involved in investing. While the *Treatise* is perhaps Keynes's least accessible work, it asks the age-old question of what can be quantified without subjective bias. Is there an objective method by which we can predict which stocks will soar, for example? How can we separate sentiment from reality using objective science? This was not specifically articulated in the *Treatise*, but it was probably entering his mind around that time:

> The judgments of probability, upon which we depend for almost all our beliefs in matters of experience, undoubtedly depend upon a strong psychological propensity in us to consider objects in a particular light. But this is no ground for supposing that they are nothing more than "lively imaginations."[3]

In this section of the *Treatise*, we see Keynes giving us a glimpse of the "animal spirits" that emerge from his great work, *The General Theory of Employment, Interest and Money*.

To understand Keynes's later ideas on market economics, you have to view his intellectual dilemma through the lens of probability. Unlike many economists of his time, he was willing to embrace "radical uncertainty," or the daunting reality that economic science was very bad at predicting the future. Markets aren't rational. They follow their own course based on behavior, not always on the ideal world of "normal" distributions.

As John Kay noted in the *Financial Times*, "for Keynes, probability was about *believability* (italics mine), not frequency. He denied that our thinking could be described by a probability distribution over all future events, a statistical distribution that could be teased out by shrewd questioning—or discovered by presenting a menu of trading opportunities."[4]

In other words, Keynes saw that statistics could *describe* the present and the past, but wouldn't necessarily predict the future. In keeping with what Mark Twain said, that there are "lies, damned lies, and statistics," Keynes didn't see an economic world that could be depicted accurately by numbers alone. Past was *not* prologue. There was also subjective reality, the little gremlin in our heads that could find a pattern in any set of numbers that would fit a pet theory. Yet how can we separate our feelings from the rigorous rules of monetary theory, supply and demand, and other strictures of classical economics? How is behavior involved? To answer that question, Keynes had to explore the nature of the behavior beast, which became a fascinating part of his 1910 lectures.

The Beast of Speculation: Lectures Before World War I

Before World War I, Keynes's activities in the stock market were limited. Since he didn't have inherited wealth (and lecturing at Cambridge didn't pay that much at the time), he was dependent upon allowances (roughly $160 each) from his father and his mentor, Alfred Marshall, and upon tutoring fees. Although he managed to accumulate money received on birthdays and from academic prizes in a "special fund" started in 1905, he didn't really start investing in earnest until 1914, according to the editor of his papers, Donald Moggridge. Prior to that point, he'd only dabbled in a handful of stocks.

"By 1911, he was not only buying additional shares, but also making switches and helping manage certain family trust funds," Moggridge discovered.

PORTFOLIO SNAPSHOT

Early Stock Holdings—Buying on the Way Down and Dollar Cost Averaging

In this small sampling of Keynes's personal portfolio prior to World War I, we see how he was buying and selling one of his favorite stocks at the time: U.S. Steel. (He also owned longtime favorite Mather & Platt, an engineering firm, and Marine Insurance.) He consistently purchased shares at lower prices, thus reducing his average cost. The 20 shares he sold (in this sample) were at prices within 10 percent of the highest purchase price.

This is a tried-and-true method called "dollar cost averaging" that has worked for individual investors for decades because it avoids buying at the absolute highest price and selling at the lowest. It is a good method for long-term buy-and-hold investors who want to own companies that offer dividend reinvestment plans, through which new shares can be purchased at no commission. If Keynes liked a stock, he kept buying it and was encouraged when the price came down, so he bought more and got better bargains.

Year	Shares/Price
1911	10 @ 71¾
1912	10 @ 60¾
	10 @ 66¾
	20 @ 66¾
SELL	10 @ 68⅜
	10 @ 65
1913	10 @ 66⅓
	20 @ 65¾
	30 @ 65¾
	30 @ 61½
	30 @ 62
SELL	10 @ 67
	20 @ 59½
	20 @ 60³⁄₁₆

High = 71.75; Low = 59.50
Number of shares bought = 220; average price = 64¾

Number of shares sold = 20; average price = 67⅔
Average of all transactions = 64.09 (rounded off and decimalized)
Source: Keynes's personal ledgers and Buckmaster & Moore brokerage state-
ments, King's College archives.

Keynes managed to build his knowledge through experience,
book learning, and teaching. Even at Eton, it was clear to his
teachers and fellow students that he was an extraordinarily quick
study. Though he was probably teased for his intellect and his features (his nickname was "Snout"), he was able to master complex
concepts with ease. This built his confidence and allowed him to
venture into areas in which he had no formal training. It also
helped that he was great at math.

One of his passions became investing, although none of his
academic training prepared him for this activity. At the time,
there were no such things as money management programs or
Chartered Financial Analysts. And if anyone was managing institutional money, the technique was pretty straightforward: *you
bought and held bonds.* So when Keynes discovered the world of
the stock, commodity, and currency markets—probably through
his association with stockbroker Oswald Falk—it must have
been exhilarating. Here was a venue for his Promethean analytical skills, aided and abetted by his love of gambling. Being
a confident young man, he must also have had the sense that he
could calculate some pretty good bets, considering that his main
academic interest at the time was probability. Although it's not
known which attitudes he conveyed to his students in his lectures
and Economic Club meetings, it's clear that he was developing a
fervent passion for investing before the Great War.

In a proper English mien, though, Keynes wanted to impress
upon his students that there were important differences between

investing (pretty much buy and hold), speculation, and gambling. In his 1910 lectures, he made those distinctions fairly clear. Here are his definitions:

♦ **Speculation.** "The essential characteristic of speculation . . . is superior knowledge. We do not mean by this the investment's actual future yield . . . we mean the expected *probability* of the yield. The probability depends upon the degree of knowledge in a sense, therefore it's subjective. If we regard speculation as a reasoned effort to gauge the future from present known data, it may be said to form the reins of all intelligent investing."[5]

♦ **Gambling.** Keynes draws the line by noting that gambling isn't based on specific knowledge or reasoning, yet he voices "considerable sympathy for the bookmaker. . . . They work as hard for their money as human beings can do, and their earnestness is remarkable. Thoughtful men of few words, they are as grave as judges, as reflective as metaphysicians and as pious as bishops; whatever their faults may be, they cannot be accused of frivolity or not working for their money."[6]

♦ **Evils of speculation.** While Keynes doesn't initially make a moral judgment on speculation, he notes the harm it could cause "through the manipulation of the market through dishonest means." He's referring to seemingly ill-gotten gains by buying, selling, or shorting securities without regard to other market players or the fundamentals behind a security's pricing.

♦ **Methods of speculation.** In speaking of dealing in "promises" to buy or sell a stock, bond, or commodity, Keynes is referring to futures and options when he states, "A man who sells a promise is a bear and one who buys a promise is a bull. In the case of stocks and shares, not promises, but actual delivery is required." (More on this in the next chapter.)

Within five years of giving these lectures, Keynes was practicing (and often ignoring) what he was preaching. On the eve of the war, there was a tremendous speculative boom, so Keynes began to apply his insights to buying and selling currencies.

As his popularity with students grew, Keynes took a greater role in the governance of King's College. He was appointed to the Estates Committee in 1911 and started to understand how the college managed its money and property. Keynes quickly challenged the fact that King's kept large cash balances; he wanted to see the money put to work. Gradually winning over his colleagues, he eventually revolutionized the management of the institution's money—and that of institutions across the world.

At the time, he was also at work writing *Indian Currency and Finance*, which was finished in 1913 and led to his appointment to a government commission.[7]

The years before the war afforded Keynes a new bevy of luxuries while his social life at Cambridge and Bloomsbury went into high gear. He took several vacations, visiting Greece, Sicily, Italy, and France. He played golf, gambled at Monte Carlo, and collected books and art. As his income grew, so did his propensity to indulge in the life of a bon vivant. While suffragists were chaining themselves to railings, Keynes also dabbled in liberal politics (the Labour Party was just being formed), and he edited the *Economic Journal*. He moved between the sophisticated worlds of the Fabian socialists (George Bernard Shaw was their literary lion) and the bohemian Bloomsbury set, which included Virginia and Leonard Woolf, Lytton Strachey, and Vanessa Bell. Whatever Bloomsbury was, it certainly wasn't the status quo. If it had flourished during the 1960s, it would have been hippie-like in its abandonment of conventional mores. Gay love was virtually on a par with heterosexual love. All Victorian notions of behavior, worldview, and culture were being thrown out the window. Keynes was one of the leaders of this revolution, which nearly crashed and burned with the onset of World War I.

The Great War: Trashing the Treaty

Keynes gained an exemption from being sent to the killing fields of France because of a Treasury appointment, which was made in 1915. Whitehall demanded dedicated men with expertise in money, currencies, and finance to handle payments for materiel. Keynes was a natural candidate to help manage Britain's finances; he had gotten his feet wet in the India Office, and his writing had elevated his profile within the government. What Britain needed was to keep the money flowing and to aid her allies. Russia and France transferred gold to the Bank of England. Once the Dardanelles was opened, Russia would boost her wheat exports. Britain loaned money to France.[8]

Shortly after his appointment, Keynes suffered an appendicitis attack, underwent an appendectomy, then contracted pneumonia. In fact, he suffered from various ailments throughout his life, and he was constantly working, even on vacations. When the war ended, he was assigned to advise the Treasury on the Versailles Treaty, but he vehemently disagreed with the reparations that were being extracted from Germany. Based on his knowledge of exports, currency, and industrial production, he believed that Germany would be economically crushed by what France, Britain, and the United States were demanding, so he left his post and began writing a book that would change the way civilizations behave after a war. Its influence is still being felt today.

Economic Consequences: Rebel with a Cause

Keynes's insight into the potential destructiveness of the Versailles Treaty was not shared by those who were drafting the treaty.

When he published *The Economic Consequences of the Peace* in 1919, it was soundly attacked by the British establishment. After all, wasn't it the role of a victor to demand humiliating payments from the loser? Couldn't you *economically* avenge the cost of millions of lives lost? Keynes thought this was a horrible concept that would destroy what was left of the once-robust German economy. In the book, Keynes not only savages the victors, but lays out a rational case for how channeling excessive payments from a devastated German people would not work. Germany could not possibly export enough goods to pay the reparations, Keynes calculated. In the final analysis, it would be a "lose-lose" situation for all parties involved and certainly would not cement the peace. The leaders of the time were infuriated with Keynes, who had broken one of the ironclad rules of being an elite British civil servant: not telling tales out of school. Although Keynes had flexible personal views on morality, it was clear that *Economic Consequences* was a masterwork of economic ethics. Why make a country shoulder the price of something monumental if it will never be able to pay you?

Robert Skidelsky saw *Economic Consequences* as a turning point in the evolution of Keynes's intellect. The economist had bolted headlong into the world of diplomacy, history, and moral reasoning. The "war to end all wars" would be nothing of the sort.

> He had spoken like an angel with the knowledge of an expert. This mastery of science and words was to be the basis of all of his achievement. But there was something else. Keynes not only asserted his claim to attention but the claim of economic science to shape the future. The princes of the old world had left a dreadful mess; it was the task of the scientists to clean it up. This was a message with a powerful appeal to a rising generation.[9]

While mentors like Moore and Marshall were revered in their own little worlds, Keynes now vaulted onto the world stage. His book became a bestseller on both sides of the Atlantic, and he morphed into a superstar in a world that had ravaged and disintegrated dynasties from Moscow to Vienna. The old world had come apart as Keynes was coming together. Not only did he dismantle the treaty in *Economic Consequences*, but he laid out a future economic scenario for Germany if it was imposed: "the menace of inflationism."[10] As history tells us, inflation was the financial calamity that led to the fall of the Weimar Republic and the rise of Hitler.

Despite all of his warnings and economic figures showing the ultimate impact of the treaty, Keynes closes the book—and the era—with a prosaic aside that underscores his growing manifesto for compassionate capitalism:

> In this autumn of 1919, in which I write, we are at the dead season of our fortunes. The reaction from the exertions, the fears and the sufferings of the past five years is at its height. . . . Our power of feeling or caring beyond the immediate questions of our own material being is temporarily eclipsed. The greatest . . . events beyond our own direct experience and the most dreadful anticipations cannot move us.[11]

Nearly a decade and a half before he coined his immortal descriptive phrase "animal sprits," Keynes is posing a behavioral dilemma. He has laid out a rational case for what will happen to Germany under the treaty and stated numerous reasons for opposing it. Yet rational economics and the irrational brutality of vengeance and greed are at opposite poles of the human soul. Although the power elite had ignored him, Keynes had laid the groundwork for a body of thought that would attempt to defy irrationality, so he went on with his life, returning to Cambridge but finding a new passion: speculating with his newfound wealth.

KEYNESIAN KEYSTONES

The Currency Markets

Is speculation in currency a good way to make money? For most people, it's still as risky as it was when Keynes was engaging in it. Currency markets are notoriously volatile. Even if you believe that your macroeconomic view will prevail—as Keynes did—you're trading against all the largest institutions in the world, and they have much better information than you do. As I've noted, even if you're the most brilliant economist in the world, you can still make bad trades and get burned. If you want to do currency *hedging*, your best approach would be to invest in an emerging markets exchange-traded fund like the iShares MSCI Emerging Markets Fund (EEM). You can also hedge nearly every major currency risk through exchange-traded funds, but don't expect these vehicles to act like stocks or bonds. They don't pay dividends, and they make money only on valuation differences between currencies. Dollar cost averaging with stock purchases, however, still makes a world of sense. If you choose to buy individual stocks that have earnings and dividend-paying potential over time on a regular basis, you will not get nailed by buying too high. In fact, you can buy more shares if the price drops. This is a cornerstone of value investing, which we'll explore in more depth in coming chapters.

2

Economic Consequences

What can be added to the happiness of a man
who is in health, out of debt, and has a clear
conscience? To one in this situation, all accessions
of fortune may properly be said to be superfluous;
and if he is much elevated upon account of them,
it must be the effect of the most frivolous levity.

—ADAM SMITH, *THE THEORY OF MORAL SENTIMENTS*[1]

KEYNES SPENT HIS THIRTY-SIXTH BIRTHDAY SICK IN BED IN PARIS, missing a stunning London performance of the Diaghilev ballet *Boutique Fantasque* starring the ballerina Lydia Lopokova, a petite dynamo who would later completely captivate him. His world seemed revitalized, emerging like a phoenix from the relentless slaughter of the war. In 1919, Bloomsbury was a center of the cultural revolution that was burgeoning in the salons of Paris and London; Keynes's lively rooms at 46 Gordon Square welcomed Nijinsky and Picasso while Keynes and his friends wrote, painted, and conversed about how the world could be remade. Prior to the success of *The Economic Consequences of the Peace*, Keynes lived modestly—certainly not as well as he would have liked. As an academic, he found that money was in short supply, so he decided to take a new route and pare his university commitments. His student and first biographer, Roy Harrod, noted that "by temperament, he was courageous and always ready to take risks . . . one who had managed the external finances of the nation during the war would surely have some market value in the world of finance."[2] Yet other than his small allowances and his meager teaching salary, Keynes had no family fortune to stake his entry into the world of finance. King's College offered him the position of second bursar, which gave him access to the college's holdings, but it wasn't enough. Keynes wanted to cliff-dive into the markets.

When he became better known and his book and journalism income mushroomed, offers of important positions also materialized. One proposal was to chair a foreign-owned bank. He turned it down. His friend Oswald "Foxy" Falk, an impetuous stockbroker who worked in the City, secured an invitation for Keynes to join the board of the National Mutual Life Assurance Society, which he accepted. From 1921 through 1938, Keynes served as chairman of the insurer and managed its money. Although Keynes introduced his investment innovations to Mutual and another insurer (Provincial Insurance) over the next two decades, another role held more appeal for Keynes: speculator.

When royalties from *Economic Consequences* started to pour in, Keynes was flooded with speaking requests, even as he was still being widely denounced in official circles for his vexing attack on the Versailles treaty. He became flush with cash and in demand as a journalist, writing for the *Nation*, the *Manchester Guardian*, and the *New Republic*. The rest of Europe, though, was struggling. People in Germany were starving, and the end of the war brought on not only a recession, but the great flu pandemic, which began in 1918 and took the lives of some 40 million people across the world.[3] Economically, the slump hit both sides of the Atlantic as the world was sorting out the new world order.

Currency Speculation

Using his knowledge of international finance, Keynes took to the currency markets with abandon. Currencies had been fixed before 1914, but now were floating and notoriously volatile, but Keynes thought he had the advantage of "superior knowledge." Believing that postwar inflation would hurt the values of the French franc (1924 and later), the German reichsmark (in circulation from 1924–1946), and the Italian lira (currencies that continued to exist until the time of the eurozone integration), Keynes shorted those currencies. (These transactions would make money if the currencies dropped in value relative to other, stronger currencies, such as the British pound and the U.S. dollar.) He went long on the Indian rupee, the Norwegian and Danish kroner, and the dollar.

"He wanted to make money in a hurry in the 1920s," his biographer Robert Skidelsky told me, "and thought gambling on currencies (when currencies were floating in the early 1920s) was the way to do it."[4]

Along with Falk, his brother Geoffrey, and some of his Bloomsbury friends, Keynes set up an investing syndicate in 1920 (see the sidebar "Portfolio Snapshot: The Syndicate, 1920–1922"), which many financial historians claim was one of the first hedge funds. Rather than managing money for the preservation of capital or for yield, Keynes was speculating pure and simple. At first, his strategy paid off, netting $30,000 for his investors in the first few months. By April 1920, notes Liaquat Ahamed in *The Lords of Finance*, Keynes had made an additional $80,000, which was astounding considering that most of Europe was essentially broke from the war. Then something unexpected happened: "Suddenly, in the space of four weeks, a spasm of optimism about Germany briefly drove the declining European currencies back up, wiping out their entire capital."[5]

WHAT IS A HEDGE FUND?

While the concept of a hedge fund is rather vague, the principle behind it is employing a focused strategy without regard to diversification. Unlike traditional pension or retirement portfolios, which maintain a specific mix of stocks, bonds, and alternative investments, hedge funds can dive into specific investments and use trading strategies that are often unconventional. Some hedge funds, for example, target companies that are distressed or ripe for a takeover, while others may target interest-rate or currency swings. Other more conservative funds aim for a "market-neutral" absolute return that may produce a positive return no matter what economic conditions are at the time. In Keynes's case, he thought he could make money by taking advantage of currency swings after World War I. He had access to a wealth of information through his government relationships, so he believed that he had an insider's edge. In a nutshell, hedge fund managers are convinced that they can make money because they are concentrating on small niches in an array of markets. They are typically high-risk and expensive vehicles, usually catering to high-net-worth individuals and institutions. Over time, though, you have to weigh the success of their performance against the risk they take and the fees they charge. Very few managers are consistently profitable.

Keynes's doting father, Neville, came to the rescue and bailed out his now-middle-aged son with a "birthday present," while

Keynes himself secured a loan from the financier Sir Ernest Cassel. Keynes was back in the game; by the end of 1922, he had \$120,000 in his account.[6] That was nearly \$1.7 million in inflation-adjusted (2013) dollars. Keynes could have retired at that point, but he was emboldened. Over time, he was right about the long-term prospects of the currencies he had targeted in his short sales, but he got burned in the short run. In his pitch to Cassel, although Keynes humbly admitted, "I am not in a position to risk any capital myself, having quite exhausted my resources," once again he flashed his confidence. "I anticipate very substantial profits with very good probability if you are prepared to stand the racket for perhaps a couple of months."[7]

Not only did Keynes jump back on the speculation steed, but he was able to repay all of his investors by the end of 1922 and sat on a small profit. Now he turned his sights on the even more volatile commodity markets.

PORTFOLIO SNAPSHOT

The Syndicate, 1920–1922

This was Keynes's first significant investment venture managing other people's money, a virtual hedge fund he managed for friends and family that included his father, his sister Margaret, his brother Geoffrey, Duncan Grant, Basil Blackett, Vanessa Bell, A. V. Hill, W. Langdon Brown, and Sir Ernest Cassel, who had bailed Keynes out with a loan in mid-1920 after Keynes realized currency losses that essentially wiped out the portfolio. According to Donald Moggridge, one of his biographers, Keynes lost money in every currency position when the syndicate was closed out. He repaid his investors after jumping back into the markets from the end of 1920 through 1922. Keynes regained some of his money—reporting a negative net worth in 1920 and net assets of £21,558 in 1922.[8]

Stocks Held
London & Southwest Railway, Penarth Harbor Dock & Railway, Castner Kellner, Southhampton Gas/Light, Railway Share Trust, Foreign/Colonial Investment Trust, Bolckow Vaughan.

Commodities Traded
Metals, cotton.

Currencies Traded
U.S. dollar, French franc, Italian lira, German reichsmark (and its predecessor the "papiermark"), Indian rupees.

Source: King's College Archives; Collected Writings of John Maynard Keynes (London: Macmillan, 1971–1989), Vol. 12, pp. 4–8.

Monetary Reform and Inflation's Curse

As an exhausted England endeavored mightily to regain its prewar eminence in the world economy, Keynes was focusing on monetary reform. After the war, there was an extensive discussion of bringing back the gold standard, that is, linking the value of the pound to a specified amount of the pale metal. Keynes opposed the move, calling gold "a barbarous relic." He did, however, share the goal of bringing stability to the foreign exchange market. As he had found as a speculator, currency values had wild gyrations and huge impacts upon entire countries. He realized that fluctuations helped some while hurting others, often unequally. As he had predicted in *Economic Consequences*, Germany was being hit the hardest in the 1920s. German wholesale prices, which he charted in his 1924 book *A Tract on Monetary Reform*, had risen 765,000 percent from 1913 through

1923, ending with destabilizing hyperinflation.[9] In fact, every major country was being ravaged by inflation. Prices in England nearly tripled before receding in 1920. French prices soared by a factor of five. Even American prices more than doubled during that period.[10]

When Keynes took an incisive look at what inflation would do to the war-ravaged European economy, he believed that the currencies of Germany, France, and Italy would collapse. He was right in the short term, but confidence in a rebound triggered an upward movement in those currencies, which led the overconfident and overleveraged Keynes syndicate to tank. Inflation was *still* the enemy in a general economic sense, although markets can react to it in varying ways that are not always predictable. What Keynes would later call animal spirits—volatile herd movements of mass psychology—foiled his speculative venture.

Keynes didn't mince words when it came to the punishing impact of inflation (which was often followed by deflation) and monetary instability. In the early 1920s, he called the economic chaos and fluctuations in the value of money "one of the most significant events in the economic history of the modern world." He was concerned about the "unprecedented violence" of the volatility:[11]

> Inflation redistributes wealth in a manner very injurious to the investor, very beneficial to the business man, and probably, in modern industrial conditions, beneficial on the whole to the earner. Its most striking consequence is its *injustice* [italics his] to those who in good faith have committed their savings to titles to money rather than to things.[12]

If you're in business, as Keynes observed, you can raise your prices for the goods and services you sell. Wage earners would

probably see higher salaries. Those producing or selling commodities like agricultural products or metals would also benefit from
rising prices. But those who kept their money in the bank or
held bonds? They would suffer the most, since the value of what
they are holding in real terms (that is, after inflation erodes the
value of money) falls; they don't benefit at all from rising prices.
Ultimately those who are saving (and not speculating on currencies or commodities) get burned by doing what they think is the
right thing.

Keynes was troubled by this disparity, but he didn't think that
Britain's returning to the gold standard would remedy it. He also
thought that current economic theories on the quantity of money
were inadequate and failed to address the damage done by the
inflation-deflation cycles. Irving Fisher, the famous Yale economist, was the main proponent of the quantity theory; it stated that
there was a positive relationship between changes in the money
supply and the price of goods. That means that pumping up the
amount of money in circulation can produce inflation.[13]

Keynes's discussion in the *Tract* leads to one of his most famous
quotes. In examining the relationship between the amount of
money in circulation and its purchasing power, Keynes went
back to the period after the American Civil War, when the dollar
was stabilized, then devalued 10 percent (during the war, both
sides had printed a lot of paper money to finance the conflict).
Unhappy with the rearview-mirror economic view of the time,
Keynes voiced frustration over the economic theory of *his* time
and perhaps the failure of macroeconomics to predict when harmful cycles begin and end.

> *In the long run*, we're all dead. Economists set themselves too
> easy, too useless a task if in tempestuous seasons they can only
> tell us that when the storm is long past the ocean is flat again.[14]

Even today, although economic forecasts are published daily, one of the most important economic observations—whether or not an economy is in recession—is rarely made in real time. The National Bureau of Economic Research, for example, which makes these pronouncements for the United States, has to look backward at several measures of economic activity before it can make a call on a recessionary period.[15]

Before dispatching the suggestion that returning to the gold standard will stabilize prices, Keynes takes a side trip into "forward" or futures contracts and their relationship to "spot" or current prices of currencies and commodities. It's here that we see Keynes's practical interest, as he had been speculating for years. But the economic theorist in Keynes becomes a pragmatist in his *Tract*.

> Therefore I regard the stability of prices, credit and employment as of paramount importance, and since I feel no confidence that an old-fashioned gold standard will even give us the modicum of stability that it used to give, I reject the policy of restoring the gold standard on pre-war lines.[16]

While the idea of linking currencies to gold reserves has never lost favor in certain ultraconservative economic circles, Keynes saw that it wasn't the answer to inflation. In a dynamic economy, you need to be flexible with the money supply and credit. You may need to borrow during recessions to stimulate economic activity and pull back when tax revenues make the national treasury flush. His thinking in the 1920s foreshadows what he would tackle with vigor in *The General Theory of Employment, Interest and Money* a decade later.

What Keynes presents in the rarely read *Tract* is a worldview in which inflation and economic instability, two subjects that would occupy him for the rest of his life, are enemies of civilization. It's such a seminal work that even monetarists like Milton Friedman called it "his best book in economics. Even after sixty-five years [originally writing in 1989], it is not only well worth reading, but continues to have a major influence on public policy."[17]

Taking Delivery: Keynes's Commodity Speculation

As an economist who believed that he could quantify the impact of supply and demand curves, Keynes became enraptured with the idea of commodities trading in the 1920s. Europe clearly needed every kind of commodity in order to rebuild. Prices generally followed increased demand. There were opportunities for astute speculators, so Keynes started researching and writing about commodities in the early 1920s for the London and Cambridge Economic Service and the *Manchester Guardian*.[18]

Judging from Keynes's writings at the time, there were few details that escaped his attention. How many bales of cotton did America produce? What were the supplies of copper, tin, nickel, aluminum, rubber, and coal? How were they valued? Keynes absorbed a tremendous amount of information. What would later become available through massive online systems like Bloomberg and Reuters were all in paper form when as Keynes was digesting untold volumes of figures from nearly every continent.

SOME TRADING DEFINITIONS[19]

Backwardation. A situation in which futures prices are lower in succeeding delivery months.

Call option. The right to buy a certain future contract for a security, such as a stock or a commodity, at a set "strike" price in the future.

Contango. A condition in which futures prices are higher in succeeding delivery months than the nearest month. The opposite of backwardation.

Put option. The right (not an obligation) to sell a security or a commodity contract at a strike price in the future. The buyer pays a premium for this right. Puts are usually bought if a price drop is anticipated.

Spot price. The current cash price for a commodity for immediate delivery at a given time and place.

See http://www.cmegroup.com/education/glossary.html for more definitions.

Keynes saw his role in commodities speculation as a "risk bearer" or "prophet" who could take advantage of the difference between what the market indicated a commodity should be priced at based on actual supply and demand and what *he* surmised was the proper price. The market was inefficient, Keynes believed, and would consistently produce errors in pricing. A speculator could absorb the risk that producers, who were more interested in hedging prices, didn't want to take. If he was right, he stated he could "earn substantial remuneration *merely* by running risks and allowing the results of one season to average with those of others; just as an insurance company makes profits without pretending to know more about an individual's prospects of life or the chances of his house taking fire than he knows himself."[20]

When studying commodities, Keynes identified some behavioral factors that influenced commodity prices that were important to him as a speculator (he would also come to similar conclusions in the following decade when buying stocks):

- High prices may be brought about by general confidence or overconfidence in business prospects.
- There also may be famine high prices, due to a shortage of commodities in relation to purchasing power.
- High prices may indicate poverty as well as confidence.
- Curtailment of world production also can lead to high prices.[21]

When it came to commodities, Keynes was an absolute data wonk. His documenting of commodity price supplies and fluctuations fills nearly 400 pages of Volume 12 of his collected writings. Why this intense interest? He figured that if he could discern pricing patterns relative to supply and demand, he could make a fortune. And he seemed to have an endless fascination with a variety of compiled figures.

Commodities investing, as any trader will tell you, is data- and timing-driven. While there are dozens of strategies you can employ, it's basically a game that pits your hunches against the reality of market conditions. Do current grain prices reflect demand? Will a growing drought depress hog and cattle prices? Will rubber supplies be enough to match the demand for autos? Traders constantly make wagers based on disparities between cash and futures prices. Keynes used his extensive facility for probability analysis to make thousands of trades in a wide range of commodities. This is difficult for most people to do unless they have a capacity for analyzing large number sets and time bets based on ever-shifting market conditions. Did Keynes use his access to government and other economic information to gain a trading advantage? It's fairly clear that he did, although it wasn't considered insider trading at the time—and there were no laws against it. Most of the information he was examining was buried in extensive market reports. If anything, his uncanny ability to sort through thousands of pages of numbers worked to his advantage in placing and timing trades, something that most people can't do effectively.

PORTFOLIO SNAPSHOT

A.D. Investment Trust Ltd.

Essentially another hedge fund, A.D. was founded by Keynes and his associates at the British Treasury in July 1921. Keynes was a director of the fund until November 1927, when he sold all his shares. From 1923 through 1927, dividends were 10 percent annually. After Keynes left, the firm didn't survive the 1929–1932 sell-offs.[22] This was largely a commodity-oriented portfolio that focused on the rise of commodity prices in the wake of World War I. Even the stocks it held reflected the growing demand for staples like rope, metals, oil, and food. Currency speculation was also part of the mix. As the decade wore on, though, the portfolio was directed more into stocks and less into commodities and foreign exchange. As you can see, this is a classic example of what Keynes called "opposed risks," where gains in one asset class could offset losses in another. When he was losing money in commodities, for example, he was making money in stocks. If it weren't for the fact that this was a highly speculative and risky portfolio, this would be a good example of diversification that shows how holding relatively uncorrelated assets can result in overall gains. Ultimately, though, at the end of this sampled holding period, stocks were the winning asset class.

Commodities Traded
American cotton (New Orleans and New York Cotton Exchanges)

Copper, tin, zinc (spelter), and lead

Jute (India)

Lard

Linseed oil

Petroleum

Rubber

Sugar, coffee, tea

Nitrate (fertilizer component)

Wheat (United States and Canada), corn (maize)

Wool (Australia, New Zealand, and South Africa)

Stocks Owned

British Ropes, Courtalds, El Oro Mining, Francois, J. Finley, Jute Industries, Shell Oil, Wallpaper Manufacturing, Watney Combe

Breakdown of Profits by Asset Class (in £)

Years	Currencies	Commodities	Stocks
1921–1922	5,000	5,400	2,700
1922–1923	14,400	−6,400	3,600
1923–1924	−300	28,300	0
1924–1925	2,000	−15,000	14,500
1925–1926	1,500	−700	2,600
Totals	**22,600**	**11,600**	**23,400**

Source: CWK, Vol. 12, p. 32; King's College Archives.

Keynes's Commodities Trading Performance

In what probably what would lead to derision for a public figure today, Keynes speculated heavily in the markets while calling for their regulation. Keynes the reformer saw what damage unstable prices could do to producers and consumers, while Keynes the investor sought to take advantage of those prices. This Janus-like approach has perplexed those who have closely examined Keynes's career. It has also prompted a great deal of interest within the academic community since his death.

In 2010, the Italian Ministry of Education commissioned a group of economists to explore Keynes's commodities activities. While their interest was mainly in providing a framework for better regulation, these economists had to examine his trades. They were interested in how Keynes applied his market theories to his trading. One idea was called normal *backwardation*, which, in Keynes's view, provided protection against price fluctuations and earned the speculator a risk premium. In other words, he was exploiting the fact that sudden surges in demand can't immediately be met by increased supplies—that takes time. Storing commodities over time is also expensive.[23] When supply lagged demand, or vice versa, he'd place his bets accordingly, going short (anticipating a price drop) or long (anticipating a price increase) as indicated.

The Italian researchers reached many of the same conclusions that Keynes had reached when he wore his monetary reform hat: that fluctuating commodities prices were linked to global instability, financial crises, structural trade imbalances between nations, and difficulties in the international monetary system. Even today, economics professor Maria Cristina Marcuzzo notes, "In the absence of buffer stocks for commodities, and with insurance against price volatility based only on market mechanisms, the system is doomed to instability."[24]

Keynes speculated using futures contracts (the right to buy or sell a commodity at a certain price today and take delivery of that commodity at some time in the future) and options (a similar vehicle). In the 27 years that Keynes was trading commodities, his performance was mixed, his biographers and the Italian researchers concluded. His trading methods hinged on his views on probability and uncertainty. He assigned various degrees of uncertainty to the performance of each commodity—would the price rise or fall—then traded accordingly. Harkening back to his 1910 lectures, he was speculating based on what he thought was "superior knowledge" or "the means of forecasting the future superior to the ordinary."[25] Of course, even an intellectual luminary such as Keynes was unable to predict market movements with precision. His strategies shifted from short to long depending on market conditions, and it's difficult to tell how his trades did in the aggregate. Professor Marcuzzo told me that it would take more study to see how Keynes performed overall; it would involve hundreds of hours of further research because of the sheer volume of his trades.

Here is a summary of some of his positions (see the discussion that follows for individual investment insights):

* **Tin.** Keynes played the market in options from 1921 to 1930. After experiencing some heavy losses in 1924, he stayed long until the end of the year, eventually increasing his position. "Keynes's aggregate profit had topped £17,000, thanks mainly to the gains made during the 1926 boom, but, as soon as prices fell off their peak, Keynes started to lose money."[26]
* **Cotton.** Keynes stayed long on cotton for most of the 1920s, as demand had picked up worldwide during the decade. Depending upon the account and the period studied— Keynes traded through several different companies—his profit ranged from £4,970 to £6,300 from 1921 to 1929.[27]
* **Wheat.** Since Keynes was constantly buying and selling contracts, it's not clear whether he made money on wheat. Usually he would "roll over" his holdings (buy new contracts with different future dates of delivery). At the end of March 1936, he actually took delivery, something that speculators almost never do. According to Moggridge, he wanted to

measure the cubic capacity of King's College Chapel to see whether he could store it in the famous church. But he managed to sell some of it on the spot market.[28]

What can we learn from Keynes's commodities trading? It's not a game for amateurs, although he certainly was never trained in it. You have to have extensive information on market conditions and the ability to execute trades at the right time to take advantage of pricing inefficiencies. It's certainly not a game for novices or for conservative, buy-and-hold investors. It requires an ability to digest and analyze a steady stream of information and the timely insight to see the best trade—that is, going long or short or engaging in more complex transactions.

The Crushing Blow: Collapse in Demand

How did Keynes do overall in commodities? While it's difficult to tell because he traded so many contracts in the 1920s, Skidelsky found that in 1927, his net assets totaled more than $3.4 million (in 2013 dollars). But everything in world markets began to change in 1928, when prices began to drop and he was still long in rubber, wheat, cotton, and tin. After the stock market crash of 1929, he eventually lost some 80 percent of his net worth, forcing him to put some of his paintings on the market (he ended up not selling them).[29]

By the end of the decade, Keynes's foray into commodities ended much the same way as his move into currencies in the early 1920s, only worse. He was on the wrong side of most of his trades when demand collapsed. By 1930, after Wall Street had crashed and the world had plunged into the Great Depression, wholesale prices had plummeted 20 percent. Many commodities—wheat, cotton, wool, silk, sugar, rubber, and metals—took a 50 percent hit.

In noting this "catastrophic fall in the prices of principal primary commodities" in a brief piece in the *Christian Science Monitor*, Keynes didn't mention that the fall had also devastated *his* portfolio. Nevertheless, he knew what it meant for the world economy:

It is a disaster of the first order, for it renders the whole structure of established money incomes and many other forms of money payment inappropriate to the price level. It ruins innumerable producers throughout the world, and has brought somewhere between 10 and 20 percent of the world's normal business activities to a standstill.[30]

Not even Keynes had foreseen the arrival of the behemoth that was going to devour the world economy in the 1930s and lead to World War II. On the eve of the 1929 crash, Keynes's popular American counterpart Irving Fisher proclaimed that "stocks had reached a permanently high plateau." One of the greatest bubbles in history exploded like an atom bomb, blasting everything in its economic path, from stocks to commodity prices. Keynes's "superior knowledge," which consisted of mountains of pricing data, failed to save his portfolio. But he dusted himself off and started anew in one of the worst decades in economic history. Once again, he learned from his predictive shortcomings and evolved into a different kind of investor.

KEYNESIAN KEYSTONES

Why Commodities Are Still Dangerous

Before the great crash of modern times ravaged investors and economies across the globe in 2008, it was thought that commodities were a great way to diversify a portfolio. After all, growing world population and a voracious demand from China and the rest of the developing world was creating an unprecedented demand for commodities. Among other things, a growing Asia wanted coal for electricity, iron ore for steel, and petroleum to run its ever-expanding fleet of vehicles. As a result, hundreds of managed commodity funds came on the market in the early part of the twenty-first century.

One of the most popular retail funds—the PowerShares DB Index Commodity Tracking Fund (DBC)—tracked an index of commodities. Instead of buying and selling individual futures contracts, you could hold a basket of commodities that ranged from petroleum products to agricultural products. You didn't need to make single bets the way Keynes did. But as Keynes discovered after 1929, when global demand tanks, all ships get sucked into the vortex. In 2008, when stocks (as tracked by the S&P 500 Index) plunged 37 percent, a broad commodities index tracked by Morningstar lost 42 percent. Since it was holding a basket of commodities, the PowerShares fund lost nearly 32 percent in that year.[31] The harsh reality is that commodities are still incredibly volatile, often move in lockstep with stocks, and plummet when the demand picture looks bearish. While it still makes sense to have some commodities exposure, since commodities also track price inflation, it's best in the long term to own dividend-paying stocks of commodity producers or distributors. As markets become increasingly globalized, commodities will become even more linked to economic growth, most of which is likely to occur in Asia, Africa, and South America. If growth slows among the major consumers—the United States, Europe, China, or India—commodities prices will follow that trend. Keep in mind that commodities pay no dividends, have no earnings, and will continue to be among the riskiest investments to own.

3

Macro Versus Micro: The New Treatise on Money

> Mr. Hoover's first step was out of the later works of John Maynard Keynes. Precisely as Keynes and Keynesians would have advised, he announced a cut in taxes. . . . These were dramatic reductions, but their effect was sadly mitigated by the fact that for most people the taxes being cut were already insignificant.
>
> —JOHN KENNETH GALBRAITH, *THE GREAT CRASH: 1929*[1]

KEYNES NERVOUSLY WATCHED THE FRENZY ON WALL STREET from 1927 through the fall of 1929. Although he wasn't heavily invested in American companies, his partner Oswald Falk was; he had pulled out in 1928, then catastrophically reentered the following year. Up until the crash, Keynes's life was following a pattern that was common for a respected gentleman: a country home in Tilton and frequent social events in Bloomsbury featuring the great artists, writers, and dancers of the day. Nearly a decade earlier, he had fallen in love with the Russian ballerina Lydia Lopokova. They married in July 1925, after Lopokova had finally managed to extricate herself from a loveless marriage. Keynes's former lover Duncan Grant was a witness. Although Keynes's Bloomsbury friends didn't approve of Lopokova's mischievous ways and her frequent mangling of proper English, Keynes didn't much care. Virginia Woolf, in noting how the ballerina had transformed the great economist from a promiscuous lover of men to a settled, heterosexual married man of ideas, saw that he was "passionately and pathetically in love." In their charming letters during an affair that began in the early 1920s, their pet names were *pupsik* (Keynes) and *Lydochka*.[2] She brought whimsy, stability, and tireless devotion to the constantly preoccupied workaholic Keynes, who was on the verge of losing another fortune as the 1920s spiraled into cataclysm.

Keynes knew that something was afoot in 1928 as he watched money streaming into Wall Street and commodity prices fall. He was long in cotton, corn, and tin, yet he was concerned that the U.S. Federal Reserve was not doing the right thing in raising short-term interest rates to curb speculation. As Lydia prepared to dance with George Balanchine and Anton Dolin, Keynes watched the economic calamity when Wall Street began a serious of record-breaking sell-offs beginning in October 1929. When the *New York Evening Post* phoned Keynes for a comment after the first round of Wall Street's greatest debacle, Keynes proclaimed, "With low interest rates, enterprise throughout the world can get going again . . . commodity prices will recover and farmers will find themselves in better shape."[3]

Like Herbert Hoover, Keynes initially held the view that the crash simply represented the abrupt end of a business cycle, a short-term downturn that would soon pass. A few adjustments in taxes and short-term interest rates and things would be back to normal. Almost no one foresaw what transpired next. Wholesale prices tanked in 1930 across the board, effectively wiping out Keynes's commodity positions. The frenetic speculation that from 1927 to 1929 had convinced nearly everyone that he should own stocks now became a tsunami that drowned investors with margin calls and worthless share certificates. Russell Cooke, a former student of Keynes's and codirector at National Mutual, was financially ruined by mid-1930 and shot and killed himself that July.[4]

That year, Keynes managed to publish his voluminous *A Treatise on Money*, which was mostly based on the economy of the 1920s. Unlike his classic *General Theory of Employment, Interest and Money*, it offered almost no insight into what had happened in 1929 and how to fix a global economy that had run aground. The book gained some attention, although only a fraction of the notoriety he had received for *Economic Consequences of the Peace*. He was appointed to a government economic advisory council and was once again consulted on his macroeconomic insights. He was center stage again, arguing his views on monetary policy and economic recovery. Did low interest rates matter when reviving a devastated economy? What needed to be done to revive demand, restore employment, and stem deflation? Was there anything that the government could do to intervene in what had become much more than a mere correction at the end of a credit cycle?

The *Treatise* and Credit Cycles

When the crash and the Great Depression that followed it unmoored the world, it was clear to Keynes that classical economics would be forever upended. There was something irrational about the downward spiral, with *everything* from commodities to stocks plunging at once. The groundwork he had laid in *A Tract on Monetary Reform* in the mid-1920s became the scaffolding for a study on the history of money in the *Treatise*. Keynes examined the history of money and monetary policy, inflation and deflation, and savings and investment. What makes people spend during one period and save during another? What changes the value of money? How important is the supply of money? As the godfather of macroeconomics, Keynes was always interested in the global view.

Since the 1920s, Keynes had believed that cycles of credit expansion and contraction closely tracked business or trade booms and busts. It was his keen observation of a host of economic factors that informed his personal investment style. He watched rates on long- and short-maturity bonds for signs of how the cycle was moving. Interest rates were usually high at the end of the cycle and low at the beginning. According to Donald Moggridge, he wanted to call what eventually became his Independent Investment Company the "Credit Cycle Investment Company."[5] Keynes employed his knowledge of cycles to time his trades in currencies and commodities, but his theories failed him in 1929. Highly leveraged when the crash came, he was forced to liquidate most of his positions, leaving a large holding of Austin Motors, which had lost three-quarters of its value from 1928 to 1929. His A.D. Investment Trust, which he had cofounded with Falk, but had left as director in 1927, folded, as his relationship with his broker friend soured.[6]

What lessons did the late 1920s hold for modern investors? Although Keynes believed that he could track credit and commodity cycles—and had more information at his disposal than most investors—he didn't foresee the crash of 1929. Just as only a handful of market observers predicted the meltdown of 2008 or the dot-com bust of 2000, the majority of investors have no idea when a bubble is ready to burst and are often long in a particular asset. That's why Keynes's formative strategy of "opposed risks," which we now call diversification, continues to make sense. Bond holdings provide a hedge against stocks. Gold, commodities, and real estate bolster portfolios against inflation. Correlations are the key in diversification. What moves in the opposite direction from stocks and other asset classes? Allocations should reflect this safety strategy.

PORTFOLIO SNAPSHOT AND AUTOPSY

P.R. Finance Company

P.R. Finance Company, which shared many of the same strategies and positions as A.D., involved Keynes to a lesser degree (he managed only one-third of that portfolio, with Falk overseeing the remainder), but you can see his thumbprint on the allocation. When Keynes and Falk thought the credit or business cycle was in an upswing, they went long on most commodities, particularly tin, rubber, and cotton. They also liked manufacturers such as Austin and Leyland Motors, railroads, and mining companies. The company, organized in 1923, included Keynes's brother and father, Falk, and several other investors who were friends or associates of Keynes or Falk. It was structured similarly to A.D. Investment Trust and was set up to increase the capital of some of the common investors. At first, the company was successful in commodity trading, which was its main investment activity. But by 1928, the firm ran aground because of its commodities speculation. After a string of losses in the 1930s, the fund was liquidated in 1935, posting a net loss of £87,653 in capital (not including dividends).[7] Although the records for this fund are incomplete, its commodities positions during a time of severe deflation proved to be the undoing of the portfolio. As was typical of many of Keynes's portfolios, there was a pronounced shift: from commodities and currencies in the late 1920s and early 1930s to stocks by the end of that decade. Also note the cross-ownership in A.D. Investment Trust.

A String of Losses (£)

1929	−30,537
1930	−50,658
1931	−15,938
1932	−1,874

Holdings

Commodities: Cotton, rubber, sugar, and wheat
Stocks: Leyland Motors, Hector Whaling, Recenia Shaerf, Islas de Guadalquivir, Francois Cementation, AD Investment, San Paolo Coffee, Teja Malaysia Tin, Southern Railway (preferred), Underground Electric Railway/London, Unilever, Austin Motor, Overseas Securities, Shell Union Oil, Select Industries, Hudson Motor, Commonwealth Southern, Montgomery Ward, Kennecott Copper, American Smelting, Swedish Match, International Nickel, American Radiator
Source: King's College Archives.

How Keynes Tracked Cycles

Cycles are always important in understanding when the tide comes in and out for investors. When is the best time to buy and sell? When should you short a position in anticipation of a lower future value? How does the general economy affect the supply and demand? Keynes eventually came to understand how the flow of money could be divined, but not completely understood, since it was always subject to some underlying rules, which he elaborated in the *Treatise*.

- **Purchasing power.** This is of paramount importance to most people. The value of money is determined by many things: the rate of current inflation, prices, currency exchange rates, and a whole host of other factors. Keynes boiled it down to this: "A man does not hold money for its own sake, but for its Purchasing Power—that is to say, for what it will buy. Therefore his demand is not for units of money as such, but for units of purchasing power."[8]

- **Savings and investment.** Keynes viewed savings as "the act of the individual consumer . . . [it] consists in the negative act of refraining from spending the whole of his current income on consumption." In his view, investment was somewhat more restricted to "the act of the entrepreneur . . . measured by the net addition to wealth whether in the form of fixed capital, working capital or liquid capital."[9] Sometimes consumers would "hoard" their money in savings during downturns, with corresponding contractions in investment by entrepreneurs. While Keynes didn't apply this thinking in the *Treatise* to the immediate postcrash environment, it would become fundamental to his *General Theory*.

- **Commodity inflation.** This occurs when the price of goods accelerates, often disobeying the laws of supply and demand. As Keynes witnessed and exploited in the early 1920s, when commodities were in great demand after World War I, prices can soar for no rational reason. "The result of commodity inflation is to cause the current output of the community to increase faster than would otherwise be the case."[10] In real terms, commodity prices raise the price of goods, but these prices eventually fall to reflect actual demand. When the global economy collapsed in 1930, that was what initially happened, cratering Keynes's commodity portfolios.

◆ **Profit.** Since Keynes was forever wedded to the idea of capitalism, he constantly observed and traded upon the interplay between thrift (saving) and investment to produce a profit. Simply put, businesspeople wouldn't invest unless they had expectations of a positive return. "Thus Thrift may be the handmaid and nurse of Enterprise. But equally she may not. . . . For the engine that drives Enterprise is not Thrift, but Profit."[11]

Toward the end of the *Treatise*, after dancing around his formative ideas on cycles, history, and monetary policy, he finally addresses the catatonic climate of 1930 and how his theories connect.

> The pessimism and the atmosphere of disappointment which the stock-market collapse engendered reduced enterprise and lowered the natural-rate of interest; whilst the "psychological" poverty which the collapse of paper values brought with it probably increased saving.[12]

Now Keynes departs from classical views of economics, foreshadowing his quantum leap in the *General Theory*. All the hidebound rules of economics were still important—saving, investment, money supply, credit—but what about mass psychology? How could one measure that, and what does it mean to society and investors? The classical view was that economies experienced shocks at the ends of cycles, then automatically corrected, like a fallen bike rider getting back in the saddle to resume pedaling. Some economists still believe that today. But the loss of 80 percent of his net worth deeply stung the proud economist. Keynes gleaned that there was something *irrational* at work, something distinctly behavioral that didn't act like part of a normal credit cycle.

The Missing Link in the Crash

The missing factor, as Keynes would later surmise but not be able to measure, was *confidence*. When banks feel confident (more on this in the next chapter and Chapter 6), they lend money to individuals and businesses because they expect a return on their money. During periods of robust employment, it seems probable that they'll get paid back. People buy homes, appliances, and cars during such periods. Businesses invest in equipment and hire more workers. At the front end of a credit cycle, money is relatively cheap. Supply and demand for goods and services are balanced. The flow of money keeps things on an even keel. There's economic growth and people keep buying things, so businesses keep hiring. Then, like a cocky teenager in a speedy car, confidence morphs into "irrational exuberance," Federal Reserve Chairman Alan Greenspan's characterization of the late-2000 dot-com bubble. If central bankers perceive that the economy is getting overheated, speculation is rampant, and asset prices (such as those of real estate or stocks) seem to be overvalued, they often raise interest rates across the board. Hopefully, the economy cools down enough to dampen speculative buying after rates rise. But central banks rarely monitor mass exuberance closely enough or react fast enough, so the adolescent economy drives off a cliff.

Charles Kindleberger, the MIT economics professor who later analyzed financial collapses in his classic *Manias, Panics and Crashes*, observed that economics during Keynes's time (and perhaps ours as well) was ill suited to describe what had happened after the 1929 crash. Keynes and his followers couldn't track "the instability of expectations, speculation and credit and the role of leveraged speculation in various assets." Most theories about crashes, Kindleberger concluded, were "incomplete."[13]

You can study the money supply in real time all you want and not reach a valid conclusion as to whether speculators are over-leveraged at certain points in time. It's *still* difficult to measure. What happened in 1929 and during other crashes was that when you are speculating with borrowed money and asset prices decline, your lenders get scared and want their money back. As a result, investors sell out positions that they otherwise would have kept, and that triggers more price drops, since other people are doing the same thing. Banks, investors, and other institutions that lent money then get burned. Credit dries up, and investment comes to a halt. In fact, in the first half of 1930, international lending briefly rebounded, but it then hit a wall when banks across the world began to fail. Banks with inadequate reserves quickly became insolvent because the money they were supposed to hold for depositors had been lent to speculators. (This was before federal deposit insurance and the numerous backstops that were afforded banks up until 2008.) Widespread panic, of course, created a chain of financial calamities as "bank failures continued to spread in a positive feedback process of falling prices, bankruptcies and bank failures," Kindleberger wrote. "Bottom was reached only with the general Bank Holiday of 1933, and the depreciation of the dollar in the spring of that year."[14]

Keynes's Portfolio Killed Again

To obtain a reasonably good picture of how Keynes's fortunes declined from the early 1920s to the mid-1930s, I examined the statements from the P.R. Finance Company (see "Portfolio Snapshot and Autopsy: P.R. Finance Company" sidebar earlier in this chapter), which he ran with Falk. After the firm lost money in 1923, the management structure placed Falk in charge of two-thirds of the fund's assets and Keynes in charge of the remainder.

The company paid dividends in 1923, 1924, and 1927, but it began to experience heavy losses in 1928 because of the fund's large commodity positions.[15]

P.R. Finance was founded in 1923 with an initial capitalization of £115,000 (each share was worth £1). The shareholders included Keynes's Bloomsbury friends Lytton Strachey and Clive Bell; Keynes's brother Geoffrey and his father, John Neville; and associates and friends of Falk's. Keynes and Falk often clashed on investment policy decisions. Falk didn't take suggestions or direction very well, and Keynes was stubborn. By the end of the 1920s, they were at loggerheads. By 1936, the company had been liquidated.

In addition to its disastrous commodity positions, however, the fund owned some U.S. utility shares (see Table 3.1), which paid high dividends for the time and held up much better than the commodity contracts. Note that all the companies paid fairly generous dividends. Private utilities, most of which were formed around the turn of the twentieth century, attracted steady investors this way because they were extremely capital intensive. As the mass distribution of power increased during the second industrial revolution—mostly made possible by high-voltage transmission lines and the alternating current system—power companies were in constant need of capital to build power plants, transformers, and lines. They eventually came to be regulated by state utility boards, which guaranteed their rates for certain periods of time. That enabled the companies to lock in high dividends for investors. (See my *Merchant of Power* for how this method of financing evolved.)

Although most of the power companies thrived, some of those that were owned by combines were linked to pyramids: holding companies that were subject to stock speculation. Many of the holding companies collapsed in the 1930s. This was the subprime crisis of the Great Depression. As a result, nearly all

TABLE 3.1   P.R. Finance U.S. Stock Holdings (1934)

Stock	Dividend (for Cumulative Preferred Shares)
American Gas & Electric	6%
American Power & Light	$5/$6
American Water Works & Electric	$6
Boston Edison	Common shares
Central & S.W. Utilities	$7
Columbia Gas & Electric	5%/6%
Commonwealth Edison	Common shares
Commonwealth & Southern	$6
Consolidated Edison	$5
Detroit Edison	Common shares
Electric Power & Light	$6/$7
Engineers Public Service	$5/$6
National Power & Light	$6
Niagara-Hudson Power	5%
North American Co.	6%
North American Power & Light	$6
Public Service of N.J.	6% to 8%
Southern California Edison	Common shares
Standard Gas & Electric	$4/$7
United Gas	$7
United Gas Improvement	$5
United Light & Power	$6

Source: Statement from P.R. Finance Co., 1936, King's College archives, JMK/PR/2.

of the combines were broken up into smaller operating units by New Deal legislation, and therefore many of these companies don't exist today, making it difficult to track their stock prices. Nevertheless, the operating companies producing power proved to be fairly durable investments because of the dividends.

The early years of P.R. Finance had gone relatively well. Losses on the most speculative positions in currencies and commodities were small, but growing. The company's balance sheets show assets of £579,552 in 1923 and £646,157 in 1924. The following year, the company was able to pay a robust 8 percent dividend to shareholders.

By the end of 1930, however, the company's capital had shrunk to £251,000, and it fell even more the following year, to £147,860, before rebounding to £491,899 by 1935.

Still, that doesn't tell the whole story because the portfolio had actually rallied in the early 1930s. When the voluntary liquidation was announced in July 1934, net assets were listed as £102,599 with profits of £81,091.[16] In investment terms, that meant that the shareholders were essentially being handed back their capital, "as the assets of the Company have now recovered to the near neighborhood of par (what they initially paid for their stakes)," the shareholders were told.[17]

A year before Keynes moved to liquidate the firm, the portfolio had managed to hold its own during the previous 15 months, being "singularly free of anxiety . . . we have suffered no serious setbacks."[18] In 1933, owing to a minor market rebound, P.R. reported a 30 percent book profit (based on the breakup value of the company's assets at the beginning of the year).[19] "This is a much more favourable result than has been attained for some time past, though the year 1932 was by no means free from risks and difficulties."[20]

Yet in the wake of a wave of crashes in 1929 and the early 1930s, P.R. Finance's portfolio was blistered. It lost £1,874 in 1931, and Keynes told shareholders, "we can indeed feel some relief to have survived such a year as 1931 without extinction."[21] Compared to the previous year, though, when the portfolio had lost £15,938; and 1929, when it had lost £50,658,[22] this performance didn't seem so bad.[23] Losing one-third of the initial capital in one year wasn't out of line with what other investors around the world were experiencing. Certainly millions either were cleaned out or chose to bail out in 1929. (Actually, the portfolio's troubles began in 1928, when commodities positions triggered a £30,537 loss.[24] That compares to a gain of £17,559 for the previous year.)

The fact that Keynes and his investors survived with any capital, given their heavy betting on commodities, was probably a testament to Keynes's willingness to hold on to the utility shares. In the face of brutal market conditions, he was probably optimistic about the *intrinsic value* of those companies, which few investors were contemplating at a time when there was blood in the streets. After all, utilities were selling something that people wanted and needed. They weren't selling precious metals or commodities that society could cut back on to a large degree. When the fund was liquidated, it was dominated by preferred American utility shares, with small holdings in commodities and currencies (see Table 3.2). What had started out as an aggressive hedge fund ended up looking like a conservative, dividend-oriented mutual fund.

Intrinsic value is a company's total value if it were to be broken up and sold tomorrow. What kind of physical assets does it own? In the case of utilities, it's power plants and transmission lines, all of which contribute in some way to revenue streams. For banks, it's deposits, loans, trading revenue, and real estate. Tangible assets make a huge difference in valuing a company and often provide a cushion when times get tough.

What Keynes Learned

Although Keynes was well known for his arrogance and his air of intellectual superiority, the humbling experience of having nearly lost two fortunes changed his thinking on the best way to invest.

TABLE 3.2   P.R. Finance Portfolio Summary
(Liquidation, Finalized July 1936)

Type	Amount
Cash on deposit with Lloyds Bank	£67
Cash on deposit with broker	£49,300
Stock	£130,058
Commodities	£982
Foreign exchange	£1,266
Pull Court Estate*	£1,321
Cruckton Estate Minerals	£914
Stock dividends	£1,171
Misc.	£789
Interest on broker cash account	£180
Total liquid value†	£186,053

* Real estate.
† Before deduction of expenses and distributions to shareholders.

The macro view of trying to guess where the economy was moving, and to link currency and commodity trades to those hunches, had failed in a big way. His new focus on confidence, sentiment, and psychology made all of his extensive research into prices, supply/demand ratios, and monetary movement seem irrelevant. Keynes's hubris, in fact, had led him down the road to overconfidence in his decisions. He held when he should have sold and sold when he should have been buying. That's one of the most common behavioral errors investors make. Most investors buy when the market rises (and assets become overvalued) and sell when prices become more attractive. It's the opposite of what you should do if you're to get the best prices.

But Keynes overcame his stubborn early views and started buying and holding more stocks. As early as 1924, he pondered the idea of shifting into equities, observing that he could reap excess return relative to bonds thanks to a "risk premium." That meant that investors were willing to take more risk in exchange for higher future returns, a bedrock principle in stock investing.[25]

As his mind shifted from that of being a short-term trader and speculator to that of being a long-term investor, Keynes began to buy stocks that he thought could weather the storm of the post-crash years. In this regard, his fortitude served him well. As his fellow investment-fund directors internalized the distress of the 1930s and urged Keynes to close out his stock positions, Keynes held fast. Here's a memo he sent to directors of the National Mutual Insurance Company, where he was managing money:

- If we get out, our mentality being what it is, we shall never get back in again until much too late and will assuredly be left behind when the recovery does come. If the recovery never comes, nothing matters.[26]
- Some of the things which I vaguely apprehend are, like the end of the world, uninsurable risks and it is useless to worry about them.
- I hesitate before the consequences of the doctrine that institutions should aggravate the bear tendency by hurrying each to be in front of the other in clearing out, when a general clearing out by the nature of things is impossible . . . and would bring the whole system down. I believe that there are times when one has to remain in the procession and not try to cut in.[27]

In the face of the worst sell-off in history, Keynes in effect became a *contrarian*. Rather than jumping into the lifeboat, he stayed on board to weather the storm. He had faith that deflation would bring back cheap money and that investors would be able to take advantage of the situation. At the same time that his commodity positions were being obliterated, he clung to the idea that stocks would not only retain some value but bounce back. It took a lot of guts to think that way in 1931, but this is what made Keynes a groundbreaking money manager and an inspiration for future investors. Yet he was just getting started in launching a whole new school of thought on investing—and economics.

KEYNESIAN KEYSTONES

The Issues with Speculation

Speculation, by its very nature, is a high-stakes game. Few succeed at it for long; even if they're convinced that they have superior insights into the future and the direction of the market. The market doesn't suffer fools gladly. It also makes little sense to believe forecasts. Even in the 1930s, events spun out of control to create a global panic that no one had predicted. This was long before electronic exchanges, high-frequency trading systems, and the Internet. Bad news on financial markets travels at the speed of light. Keynes learned that the unpredictable elements of the market are most subject to behavioral factors that can be neither measured nor fully anticipated. You're always better off knowing these risks rather than focusing on returns. Risk today can be measured in any number of ways: downside past performance, standard deviation (volatility), Sortino ratios, or downside capture ratios. All of this information is online and accessible for free. What's even more important is the company's total return based on potential appreciation and dividend payments.

Keynes's shift into dividend payers in the 1930s made a huge difference in his total return. He was buying companies that not only had steady cash flows and earnings, but were likely to *continue* to pay dividends. That's a good foundation for any stock investor. Also look for dividend *growth*, which was important to Keynes. How likely is it that a company will consistently raise its dividend to reward loyal investors? Many of the companies that Keynes bought in one of the worst investment decades in history are still around in one form or another. If anything, population growth has demanded even more power, water, and natural gas. But you need to separate the wheat from the chaff with stock purchases. As Keynes became a more focused stock investor, he realized that he preferred buying companies that were sharing a portion of their earnings in the form of dividends instead of those that were bought for mere speculation. Even if another 1929 or 2008 doesn't come along, you still need to do your homework. Ignore forecasts and gurus. Turn off the business news shows. Know how much risk you can take, and adjust your portfolio accordingly.

Building Portfolios
with Opposed Risks

I don't think I heard the name of John Maynard
Keynes until I got to Harvard. At Princeton, they taught
the famous quantity theory of money as though
they heard it directly from David Hume in 1750.
—PAUL VOLCKER, FORMER CHAIRMAN OF THE U.S. FEDERAL RESERVE[1]

"I'M IN FAVOR AGAIN," KEYNES HAD WRITTEN LYDIA AFTER A raft of government officials began asking for his advice in the wake of the 1929 crash. Although Keynes's favorite Liberal Party candidate, David Lloyd George, had been defeated by the Labourites, Keynes was optimistic that the new government would usher in a new era of cheap money to restart the economy. In concert with his Liberal Party colleagues, Keynes wanted the government to spend money to create jobs and consumer demand. However, that concept had little support from the conservatives: Winston Churchill, who was the outgoing Tory chancellor of the exchequer, disparaged the notion of what would later be called a "Keynesian stimulus." Churchill's parting words to Parliament at that time were, "very little additional employment and no permanent additional employment can, in fact, and as a general rule, be created by State borrowing and State expenditure."[2]

But the growing joblessness and despair created by the Great Depression ignored Churchill and the followers of economist Friedrich Hayek, Keynes's "Austrian school" philosophical nemesis, who had been teaching at the University of Chicago and the London School of Economics. Keynes's ideas found some currency as big-business Republicans like Herbert Hoover accelerated public works projects in the United States and his Treasury secretary, Andrew Mellon, asked Congress for 1 percent tax cuts for corporations and individuals.

Meanwhile, not only was Keynes in hot demand as the economic fix-it man *du jour*, but he was becoming a multimedia celebrity, with speeches, articles, and radio talks. While trying his best to exude optimism that the downturn would be short-lived and the Federal Reserve would enact a stimulative monetary policy, he dispelled the widely held belief that the Depression was moral punishment for the licentiousness and wild, leveraged speculation of the Roaring Twenties. He saw the crashes as more technical in nature (engines that could be fixed), employing automotive metaphors and suggesting that the global economy had "magneto" (starter) problems.

In *Grand Pursuit*, Sylvia Nasar observed that Keynes, reflecting his views in his *Treatise on Money*, thought that a central bank could "restrain or encourage investment, depending upon whether it wished to stimulate or slow economic activity. And by controlling investment, the monetary authorities could keep it in line with saving, and prices in line with costs. This is what Keynes believed in 1931, when he was still confident that concerted action to lower interest rates would end the slump."[3]

Keynes was so optimistic that he began buying American and Indian cotton again. Yet the slump proved to be stubbornly intractable as the 1930s ground on, forcing Keynes to offer for sale his prized impressionist paintings, including Matisse's *Deshabille*;[4] however, he couldn't find any satisfactory buyers. He also began to revise his entire investment philosophy.

The Birth of Opposed Risks and the Curse of Correlation

What Keynes and most other investors didn't anticipate was that in a massive sell-off, most assets other than bonds move in lockstep. Currencies, (nonrental) real estate, and commodities, unlike dividend-paying stocks, aren't backed by reserves or earnings. These tangible assets are often the first to be sold off during a crisis, even though they normally move in different directions from stocks and bonds. Since Keynes held only a small percentage of fixed-income securities in his P.R. Finance portfolio and (initially) had a large stake in commodities futures contracts, the portfolio's risk exposure was unusually high.

What buoyed Keynes and his investors to some degree in the 1930s was what the economist called "opposed risks," or the tendency for distinctly different asset classes to be uncorrelated. Later, through the work of Nobel Prize winners Harry Markowitz and William Sharpe, economists—and money managers everywhere—became able to quantify the value of having certain percentages of a portfolio in different asset classes. Through an understanding of risk variation among stocks, bonds, and other assets; Modern Portfolio Theory; and mean-variance optimization," investors could have some idea of how their portfolios would perform under various market conditions. For example, a simple portfolio that was split between 60 percent stocks and 40 percent bonds would perform better during a bear market than an all-stock portfolio, which would offer the best return during a bull market.

As Keynes would later conclude, panicked sellers who need to raise cash will dump certain assets first (like commodities) and try to hold on to vehicles that have income components. Dividends and bond payments act as a buffer during sell-offs, as investors would rather have some money coming in the door and dispense with their most speculative investments.

But the crash mentality changed everything. Prices of most commodities plummeted, since industrial production cratered as a result of lack of demand for most consumer and industrial goods. Instruments that normally moved independently of stock prices followed Wall Street closely. In a period when factories were shutting down, home and commercial construction had ground to a halt, and unemployment was soaring, commodities were the worst place to be. In 2008, it should be noted, the same lockstep decline in commodities and stocks occurred again. Global investors, correctly sensing that a widespread recession was imminent, sold commodities, foreseeing that demand would plummet.

Prior to 1928, Keynes was spot on in wagering that commodities would be in demand after World War I. That seemed like a pretty safe bet. And, even though it was some 30 years before the development of Modern Portfolio Theory, Keynes surely knew that commodity prices were *usually* negatively correlated with stock and bond prices. He had studied reams of data. Yet, even after experiencing the post–World War I recession, Keynes and most of the world was unprepared for the crash and the Depression that followed it.

COMMODITIES AND CORRELATION RISK

Surprisingly, the same theories of noncorrelation and opposed risks pervaded institutional money management in the decades prior to the 2008 crash. According to money manager and neurologist William Bernstein, "commodities exposure seemed to offer portfolio theory's version of the Immaculate Conception: high returns combined with low correlations with other standard portfolio components."[5] Here's what the correlation grid looked like, according to Bernstein (also called "Markowitz" inputs):

COMMODITIES, STOCKS, AND LONG-MATURITY GOVERNMENT BONDS (1972–1990)

	Return	SD*	GSCI[†]	S&P 500[‡]	Long Gov't
GSCI	16.26%	23.52%	1.00	—	__
S&P 500	10.99%	17.50%	−0.37	1.00	__
Long Gov't	8.49%	12.38%	−0.28	0.40	1.00

Source: William Bernstein, *Skating Where the Puck Was: The Correlation Game in a Flat World* (Investing for Adults, eBook II) (Bernstein, 2012), p. 5.

* Standard deviation, a measure of volatility and risk. The higher the percentage, the greater the price variation.

† Goldman Sachs Commodity Index, a basket of commonly traded commodities.

‡ Standard & Poor's 500 Index of the largest U.S. stocks by capitalization.

This table shows how various asset classes are correlated during noncrisis periods. As you can see, the Goldman Sachs commodities index normally has a negative correlation with stocks and long-maturity (30-year) U.S. government bonds (1.00 represents a perfect correlation, meaning that the asset prices move in the same direction). Bonds also have a low correlation with stocks. The 1920s risk scenario probably looked like this to Keynes.

Trouble with Commodities Prices

Commodities are fickle beasts, though betting on them requires an idea of how prices might move in the future and what the market conditions for specific commodities are. Futures contracts are bets that a commodity will hit a certain price by a certain date. Sometimes spot prices outpace forward or future prices, which Keynes called "normal backwardation." Then again, futures prices could exceed spot prices, a situation that is mysteriously called "contango." Generally, traders try to exploit the disconnect between cash (spot) and futures prices.

During prosperous times, Keynes used his knowledge of cotton, tin, wool, and other commodities prices to go long or short on specific contracts. The movements of those commodities followed their own path, based on supply and demand. However, when 1929 ushered in a worldwide Depression—Keynes saw signals of this in 1928—all bets were off, and suddenly nearly all commodities followed stocks into oblivion. Widespread panic triggered a rush to the lifeboats.

In our own time, as Bernstein observed, "during the 2007–2009 financial crisis, the other shoe, in the form of much higher correlations, dropped; commodities futures, rather than being a non-correlating 'alternative' asset, saw price declines just as devastating as those in equities."[6]

History, unfortunately, had created another huge repeat of this phenomenon, catching untold millions of investors in that trap—including myself, although my holdings in a commodity fund were less than 10 percent of my total portfolio. Nevertheless, I learned the hard way that "opposed risks" really boils down to having a greater portion of your assets in bonds than in stocks, real estate, and commodities. Bonds are often the only true buffers in a non-inflationary financial crisis.

Very few investors in the 1920s (or today) were aware of and prepared for what we now call "tail" risk: the chances of an extreme *global* crisis devastating entire economies. Yet even with a lack of perfect foresight and timing, Keynes managed to survive the 1930s and achieve some remarkable returns.

Keynes and Cambridge Fund Management

As an alumnus who was actively engaged in managing the investments of King's College, Cambridge, Keynes was devoted to the idea that he could do much better than previous managers. Prior to his tenure as first bursar of the college's Chest Fund, asset management was fairly simple and unimaginative. It consisted of holding bonds and real estate. When Keynes began to revolutionize money management around 1920, he convinced the college that it could open separate accounts to hold common stock, currencies, and commodities. He was appointed first bursar at the college in 1924, meaning that he had primary control over the college's investment funds. Although Keynes was technically a math major, he was persuasive in convincing the college's officials that they could earn a better return.

Although it's difficult to know exactly what Keynes bought and sold from 1928 to 1945 (he died in 1946), we do know his general investment performance, thanks to Professors Jess Chua and Richard Woodward of the University of Calgary in Canada. They profiled Keynes's performance in a paper for the *Journal of Finance*. Table 4.1 shows (a condensed version of) what they found.

By any measure, Keynes did very well over this period of time. His risk-adjusted returns were impressive, as was his performance during the years in which the U.S. market didn't do as well: in 1934, 1936–1937, 1939, 1941, and 1943. To have made money during one of the worst decades for stock returns and then during

TABLE 4.1   Performance of the King's College Chest Fund Under Keynes

Year	% Fund Return	% U.K. Mkt. Return	% T-Bill Rate	% U.S. Large Stock
1928	−3.4	7.9	4.9	43.61
1929	0.8	6.6	5.3	−8.42
1930	−32.4	−20.3	2.5	−24.90
1931	−24.6	−25.0	3.6	−43.34
1932	44.8	−5.8	1.5	−8.19
1933	35.1	21.5	0.6	53.99
1934	33.1	−0.7	0.7	−1.44
1935	44.3	5.3	0.5	47.67
1936	56.0	10.2	0.6	33.92
1937	8.5	−0.5	0.6	−35.0
1938	−40.1	−16.1	0.6	31.12
1939	12.9	−7.2	1.3	−0.41
1940	−15.6	−12.9	1.0	−9.78
1941	33.5	12.5	1.0	−11.59
1942	−0.9	0.8	1.0	20.34
1943	53.9	15.6	1.0	25.90
1944	14.5	5.4	1.0	19.75
1945	14.6	0.8	1.0	36.44
Mean return[†]	13.06	−0.11		1.56
G. mean[‡]	9.12	−0.89		
SD[§]	29.28	12.55		
Sharpe Ratio	0.385	−0.129		
Treynor Index	6.46	−1.55		
Jensen Index	14.45	−1.66		

† Arithmetic mean.
‡ Geometric mean.
§ Standard deviation.
Notes: The Sharpe index or ratio is a measure of risk-adjusted performance. Positive numbers show that the manager has performed well relative to a risk-free measure such as Treasury bond returns. The Treynor index or ratio is similar, except that it measures excess return per unit of risk. The Jensen measure, also known as Jensen's alpha, also examines risk-adjusted performance above that predicted by the portfolio's beta, or correlation to the larger market and average market return. (Investopedia, http://www.investopedia.com/terms/j/jensensmeasure.asp#axzz2 KzRyFXdZ.) The arithmetic mean, for those who need a refresher on statistics, is the sum of a set of numbers divided by the count of those numbers. A geometric mean better shows the average of percentage returns over the years indicated. While most of the table is condensed from the Chua/Woodward paper, I've added the total returns of large U.S. stocks from that period for comparison purposes as compiled by Ibbotson Associates/Morningstar.
Source: Jess Chua and Richard Woodward, "J. M. Keynes's Investment Performance: A Note," *Journal of Finance*, March 1983.

history's greatest war deserves more than a footnote in history and finance books, yet few mention it.

While Chua and Woodward didn't have full access to all the information they needed when they wrote their paper, the college told them that "all of this [investment] income was spent on modernizing and refurbishing King's College, rather than reinvested."[7] That's why King's is still one of the wealthiest colleges within Cambridge University.

More important, the results from this tumultuous period show Keynes's resilience and his willingness to adapt to changing markets. Keep in mind that during the Great Depression, there was a series of recessions followed by stock market comebacks. Although Keynes wasn't able to avoid some of the largest sell-offs (in 1930–1931, 1938, and 1940, when the Chest Fund lost 32.4 percent, 24.6 percent, 40.1 percent, and 15.5 percent, respectively), the fund had a winning streak from 1932 to 1937, a period in which U.S. stock market losses ranged from 43 to 25 percent annually. In three of those six years, large U.S. companies lost money (in terms of share price). Considering the time in which he was investing, Keynes showed either amazing skill or sizzling luck.

Looking at the three worst recorded years for large U.S. stocks (measured by total return) since 1926—1931, 1937, and 2008— Keynes did reasonably well (he was managing money during two of those years). He lost only about 25 percent in 1931, when American shares lost 43.3 percent, and he gained 8.5 percent in 1937, when U.S. stocks lost 35 percent. He beat the U.K. market in 12 out of 18 years.[8]

A More Detailed Look at Keynes's Success

More recent scholarship has taken an incisive look at Keynes's record at King's College, particularly its discretionary portfolios.

Keynes had gained the confidence of his fellows and the college administration in the 1920s, so he had a free hand to be an active investor up until his death in 1946. As I noted earlier, much of Keynes's innovative style had to do with his growing preference for stocks, although he contributed a plethora of insights and advances to institutional money management as well. David Chambers of the Cambridge University Judge Business School and Elroy Dimson of the London Business School published a landmark study in 2013 that showed that "Keynes's experience in managing the [King's College] endowment remains of great relevance today."[9] Indeed, Keynes's shift from low-yielding bonds and real estate was a key advance in institutional money management. Managers at the time knew little about how to invest in common and preferred stocks. Keynes looked at cash flow, earnings growth, and dividends with an eye toward future appreciation. With this new perspective, he was able to build wealth not only for King's College, but also for his own portfolios and two British insurance companies.

While Chambers and Dimson found that the results that Chua and Woodward had found were not that impressive Chambers and Dimson did their own study of the stocks Keynes owned for King's College—Keynes achieved an alpha of excess returns of only 8 percent and lagged the U.K. stock market during the second half of the 1920s—his outperformance was remarkable.[10] Moreover, Keynes changed his modus operandi after the crash and during the subsequent Depression. Chambers and Dimson found that the economist changed into a "bottom-up" stock picker (selecting individual stocks instead of following macro trends) in the early 1930s, a factor that contributed to his superior performance. In making this unprecedented shift, Keynes favored large companies that he could buy at bargain prices, which seeded an entire school of "value" investing.[11] Keynes's investment selections also tended to spill over to his personal portfolio, which Chambers and Dimson found contained 75 percent of the King's College holdings.[12]

Value investing, at its core, eschews a focus on macroeconomic trends. Investors searching for bargains look at what a company is likely to do several years down the road. Does it have the kind of business that will thrive in varying economic conditions? How is it insulated against or prepared for its competitors' innovations? Modern-day investors call such an advantage a "moat," implying that the competition can't easily grab market share because the cost of entry is high. Utilities and railroads are among the companies that have certain kinds of moats. It's not easy or inexpensive to build a power plant or acquire a rail right-of-way. They are likely to operate profitably well into the future. While the market may discount the share prices of these companies today, they can be bought at lower prices when overall economic conditions decline. Those who focus on value rather than the peregrinations of the broader economy can prosper over time. Keynes discovered this principle when stocks were in trouble.

What's even more remarkable is that during his heyday, Keynes was managing not only King's College's money, but institutional funds for the National Mutual Life Assurance Society (he was chairman from 1921 to 1938) and the Provincial Insurance Company (he was a director from 1923 until his death), and also personal funds for himself, friends, and colleagues.[13] Add to that his lectures, talks on the wireless, writing, active Bloomsbury social life, and advisory roles with the government, and it becomes difficult to believe that Keynes could have done all of this in one lifetime.

Keynes is believed to have been influenced in his pursuit of stocks by reading E. L. Smith's *Common Stocks as Long-Term Investments* (1924), which introduced the concept of buying stakes in companies to share in "residual claims on industrial growth."[14] Unlike a bond, which is simply a promise to pay back a debt with interest, a stock may pay its holders dividends, which are a portion of the company's earnings. In a growth environment, dividends can be increased if the company's management is sound and is expanding the enterprise. This was a radical idea for institutional investors when Keynes was managing money, although it's old hat for most value and long-term investors today. Most portfolios were restricted by rules that had been established in 1861 and were designed to preserve principal rather than pursue capital appreciation.[15] As a result, British institutions, dominated by insurance companies, eschewed equities in favor of fixed-income securities. By 1937, stock percentages had risen only to 10 percent.[16] Keynes broke the mold on the ingrained ways of institutional investing by investing the majority of his portfolios in stocks. The King's discretionary portfolios average equity allocation was 75 percent in 1922–29; 57 percent in 1930–39 and 73 percent in 1940–46.[17] Although he made a modest retreat into U.K. government bonds in the early 1930s, the "main balance" of Keynes's portfolios was invested in U.K. preferred shares, with U.S. common and preferred shares being added in the 1930s.[18]

During what would be a transformative and brutal period for money management globally, Keynes also concentrated on dividend *income*. Since he was buying common and preferred stocks that paid dividends, he sought above-average dividend yields. As government monetary policy drove down interest rates in the years following the crash, it became difficult to find decent yields on bonds. Nevertheless, his stock selection techniques identified companies that maintained high dividends, which typically meant utilities.

Keynes's concentration on dividends kept income flowing into the King's portfolios during a period in which Treasury bill rates

TABLE 4.2 King's College Income Profile

Period	U.K. Div. Yld.	U.K. Bond Yld.	King's Avg. Yield
1924–1929	5.2%	4.6%	5.9%
1930–1939	4.4%	3.4%	5.9%
1940–1946	4.0%	3.0%	5.8%

Note: The average dividend yield is for U.K. equities during those periods. The U.K. bond yield is on government securities. The King's dividend yield is on U.K. stock holdings only.

Source: David Chambers and Elroy Dimson, *Keynes the Stock Market Investor*, working paper, http://papers.ssrn.com/sol3/papers.cfm?abstract_id=2023011, p. 16.

were driven down to practically zero from 1933 to 1938, then kept below 2 percent until after World War II. He also was free to load up in a particular sector. In 1936, for example, nearly 66 percent of the King's portfolio was in mining stocks.[19] Contemporary money managers would call this a "focus" approach, where only a handful of stocks are held, as opposed to a broadly diversified or index portfolio.

Without restrictive oversight over the discretionary portfolio (Keynes had a great deal of freedom to change investment policy at King's), the economist could pick smaller stocks and companies that were linked to commodities (iron, coal, and rubber). He remained nimble in his attitude: "When facts change, I change my mind."[20]

As Table 4.3 shows, Keynes pivoted from his losing macro strategy in the 1920s, which underperformed indexes from 1926 through 1928, to a more bottom-up style thereafter. His outstanding performance reflects his modified style: he fell behind the market indexes only once in the 1930s (1938 was his worst year, but it was also dismal in the United States) and once in the 1940s. His Sharpe ratio and average performance are excellent as well.

TABLE 4.3   Keynes at King's: Performance from 1925 to 1946

Year	Discretionary Portfolio	Total*	% U.K. Equity Index	U.K. GB Index†	Rel. Perform.‡
1925	30.26%	8.54%	17.33%	3.10%	12.93%
1926	6.4	5.59	11.83	2.65	−5.43
1927	2.0	2.53	19.90	3.08	−17.90
1928	3.04	6.98	16.99	8.12	−13.95
1929	7.29	4.32	5.40	−0.31	1.89
1930	−12.48	−2.08	−17.58	9.13	5.10
1931	−5.70	−6.24	−30.17	8.03	24.47
1932	29.19	9.11	27.33	29.40	1.86
1933	54.39	34.70	27.04	5.87	27.35
1934	26.13	17.31	13.15	12.92	12.98
1935	34.75	17.39	7.95	6.71	26.81
1936	40.00	23.49	19.08	4.39	20.92
1937	11.20	4.26	0.63	−10.15	10.57
1938	−22.75	−15.06	−8.64	4.93	−14.11
1939	10.64	2.04	−5.17	−10.01	15.81
1940	−7.07	−0.24	−21.08	16.61	14.01
1941	30.55	26.67	27.24	15.01	3.31
1942	8.35	8.74	9.38	4.43	−1.02
1943	39.29	21.94	26.97	−0.49	12.32
1944	14.20	10.24	10.86	2.87	3.34
1945	12.52	9.36	3.65	12.33	8.87
1946	22.41	17.31	15.62	14.58	6.79
AM	15.21	9.41	8.08	6.51	7.13
SD	19.07	11.39	16.18	8.62	12.64
SR	0.69	0.65	0.38	0.53	N/A

* Combined return of discretionary and restricted portfolios, excluding property returns.
† U.K. government bond index return of U.K. Consols, the benchmark U.K. bond.
‡ Performance of all portfolios relative to U.K. Equity Index/DMS Total Return.
AM = arithmetic mean. SD = standard deviation. SR = Sharpe ratio. I've condensed this table to exclude restricted fund returns, although the average returns are reflected in the "total" fund performance.
Source: Chambers, D., E. Dimson, and J. Foo. "Keynes the Stock Market Investor: The Inception of Institutional Equity Investing" *Journal of Financial and Quantitative Analysis,* 2013 and Chambers, D., and E. Dimson. "John Maynard Keynes, the Investment Innovator." *Journal of Economic Perspectives,* Volume 27 Number 3, Summer 2013, pp. 1-18.

Keynes Changes Course

Toward the end of the 1930s, it was apparent that Keynes seemed to have lost faith in his earlier macro "credit-cycling" technique, which extrapolated investment returns from the flow of the business cycle. When the 1930s presented their myriad challenges, it became nearly impossible to predict when an upswing would occur. Until industrial production in the United Kingdom and the United States was ramped up to meet the demands of World War II, the global economy was fairly stagnant. Keynes also observed that credit cycling often compelled him to make bad decisions as a money manager.

> Credit cycling means in practice selling market leaders on a falling market and buying them on a rising one and, allowing for expenses and loss of interest, it needs phenomenal skill to make much out of it.[21]

As his King's College peers' confidence in him increased, Keynes acquired the freedom to improvise in his investment style. In the 1920s, when nearly every stock was rising prior to the crash, Keynes did what most investors did: he bought them on the rise. And, like most investors, he was deceived into thinking that those returns would continue and therefore overpaid for the stocks, so his performance suffered—they lost some 4 percent after the year he purchased them.[22]

Later studies by members of the growing school of financial philosophy that is now called *behavioral economics* found that investors are consistent in their patterns: they sell winners too early and hold on to losers too long (more on this in Chapter 6). That's mostly because of regret and fear of loss, according to prospect theory, developed by Daniel Kahneman and Amos Tversky.[23] Keynes, however, like a jazz musician, shifted his interpretation of how to select securities. Since his macro views on economic trends did not apply in the wretched economy of the 1930s, he refocused on individual companies. What kinds of dividends did they pay? Were they consistent? What was management like? Did he understand the company's business model? If this sounds familiar, it's because it became the mantra of the value school of investing and its major proponents, such as Benjamin Graham and Warren Buffett.

KEYNESIAN KEYSTONES

Intrinsic Value

Unlike the majority of investors, Keynes learned some invaluable lessons during the 1930s. First, owning stocks with steady dividends provides a modest buffer when the market is in turmoil. When the seas get stormy, you're going to need a lifeboat, so picking companies with solid earnings and cash flow can offset the depreciation that happens during a bear market. Keynes's flexibility during trying times was also worth emulating. You just can't stick with the same plan if it suddenly becomes painfully apparent that it's a loser. You need to be flexible.

Unlike most investors—then and now—Keynes held fast to his idea that companies had intrinsic values. He didn't judge them by their share price or by current economic conditions, which were awful in the 1930s; he carefully studied their ability to earn money over time. What made them worthy long-term investments? What kinds of dividends did they pay? He emphasized companies with steady dividends or those that had preferred payments, meaning that investors would have a steady income stream as long as the company stayed in business. Not only was this critical to his investment survival and growth during the 1930s, but it's still an essential lesson. The market is much kinder to companies that can consistently share their earnings with investors. Dividends are the "bird in the hand" for long-term investors; dividend growers are even better.

Even though he thought he could predict future economic trends, Keynes also realized that he didn't know the big picture, so he stopped trying to pretend that his crystal ball had any special powers. He refocused on examining how individual companies were managed. Would they survive the onslaught of the 1930s? How did their balance sheets look? What were their prospects for the future? Could he buy these enterprises at a good price when prices dipped? He ignored the psychologically comforting conventional wisdom that told investors to buy stocks *only* when their prices were rising. In so doing, he forced a deeper understanding of how to discover hidden value in stocks when others are panicking. It's still a worthwhile approach, and it's one that we'll explore further.

5

The Birth of Value

The Cambridge oral tradition preserves many
anecdotes about Keynes. One story has the
following exchange: "Mr. Keynes, if businessmen
are quite so stupid as you appear to believe,
how do suppose they make money?" "By
competing against each other, of course."

—PETER CLARKE[1]

By the early to mid-1930s, Keynes must have seemed like
the character John Sullivan, the dissatisfied Hollywood director
in Preston Sturges's classic *Sullivan's Travels*.[2] He was rich, moder-
ately famous, extremely well networked, and comfortable, sitting
in bed every morning scanning the financial pages for stock ideas.
Active as an arts patron, he was funding a new ballet company
in London and a theater in Cambridge. Yet he was profoundly
troubled by what he saw outside of his comfortable lodgings in
London, the countryside, and Cambridge. The laws of classical
economics weren't working the way the early nineteenth-century

economist David Ricardo and Alfred Marshall had said they would. The economy wasn't rebooting on its own to create jobs, stimulate commercial demand, and raise commodity prices. Although he was at the height of his powers—he was in constant demand as a speaker, writer, editor, teacher, and consultant—the situation was gnawing at him.

The conflict he had had with Churchill over Britain's returning to the gold standard had been resolved by 1931, when the pound was liberated from the "barbarous relic." Yet few people were going back to work and factories across the Atlantic, where the Depression raged on, were idle. The dynamo of Western commerce had gone haywire, and human misery was being compounded. When Franklin Delano Roosevelt was elected in 1932, he set the course for the New Deal, which was initially about reining in corporate power. FDR demonized industrial barons like Samuel Insull, the Chicago utilities baron.[3] By the time FDR was inaugurated in 1933, some 10,000 banks in the United States had failed. More than a quarter of the U.S. working population was unemployed. Those on the far left, such as Keynes's socialist friend George Bernard Shaw, thought that capitalism was kaput. Ever the investor, speculator, and man of ideas, Keynes knew that capitalism was not *quite* dead, but he sought to articulate why it had become so dysfunctional. His new intellectual journey not only was informed by his new economic theories, but informed his investing, creating a new paradigm.

PORTFOLIO SNAPSHOT

Keynes's Personal Stock Purchases

The following are stocks and currency positions that Keynes bought over the years for his own account, according to his personal ledgers. Unfortunately, the records don't give detailed information on what prices he sold at, but they do provide a glimpse into his ongoing pattern of buying. Many of the stocks he favored also appeared in the institutional portfolios he managed. Most of them were tied into his beliefs concerning the direction of commodity, industrial, and credit cycles. During inflationary times, he liked mining companies like Bolckow Vaughn and Rio Tinto, and also other commodity-related stocks. Even during the depths of the Depression, he saw an eventual turnaround and bought building, engineering, and manufacturing stocks. He also "ate his own cooking" by holding shares in Provincial Insurance, whose portfolio he managed.

Date Range	Stocks/Currencies
1910–1919	Eastern Bank, Harben Collins
1919–1920	Bolckow Vaughn
1914–1920	Rio Tinto, Canadian Pacific
1917–1920	Grand Trunk RR
1919–1920	U.S. dollars, Dutch florins, French francs, Norwegian/Danish kroner, Italian lire, German marks, Indian rupees
1926	Chicago Rock Island RR, Illinois Central, American Wool
1935	Associated Portland Cement, Associated Dry Goods, Atlantic Refining, Atlas, United Co.
1944	Chicago Pneumatic Tool, American Locomotive
1944–1945	Provincial Insurance, Zinc Corp., Enfield Trolley

Source: Keynes's personal ledger books, King's College Archives.

Enter the *General Theory*

With his usual swagger, Keynes wrote George Bernard Shaw in 1935 about a book "which will largely revolutionize, not I suppose at once but in the course of the next ten years—the way the world thinks about economic problems."[4] Since the 1920s, Keynes had wanted to understand the architecture of the global economy. What was the role of monetary policy? What caused prices to rise and fall during booms and busts? Why do people save at certain points in time but invest and spend at others? While he never reached any solid conclusions in his *Tract on Monetary Reform* and *Treatise on Money*, he certainly had some solid building blocks with which to create a workable economic architecture. He had always suspected that economic demand was driven by some perhaps immeasurable force. Was it the money supply? The price of gold or commodities? A businessman's expectation of return? What coalesced in his *General Theory of Employment, Interest and Money* tied together the ecology of the economy. Instead of making bold pronouncements on what would or *should* happen under rigid rules, he wanted to understand the *conditions* under which an economy went from one cycle to another.

Since the book was "chiefly addressed to my fellow economists,"[5] it's fairly certain that Keynes didn't expect his *General Theory*, first published in 1936, to be nearly as popular as his *Economic Consequences of the Peace* or his articles in the *New Statesman* or the *Nation*. It's not very accessible, and unless you're an economist specializing in monetary theory or labor economics, it's a tough book to digest without outside interpretation. It sat on my bookshelf for years; when I needed to scour it thoroughly, it still took me several passes to get through it and internalize it. Although it's considered to be a must-read by most serious students of economics, I would wager that few generalists give it a fighting chance. It's about as far from a beach book as you can get. Yet, up until MIT economist Paul Samuelson started publishing his classic textbook on economics (1948 was the year of his first edition), the *General Theory* was the Rosetta stone for postwar macroeconomics. Until Keynes and Keynesian economics fell out of favor in the 1970s and were demonized during the post-Reagan era, it was a manual for how to understand the workings of large economies. Despite its many detractors, it couldn't be more relevant, particularly for investors.

Before we go any further, keep in mind that I'm not interpreting the *General Theory* as an economist. There are a host of people with brilliant insights into his theory. The list of those who are worth reading on Keynes include Paul Krugman, John Kenneth Galbraith, Peter Clarke, Hyman Minsky, Paul Volcker, George Akerlof, Robert Shiller, Joseph Stiglitz, Jeremy Grantham, and John Bogle (the last six of whom will be revisited in Chapters 6 through 8), among hundreds of others who have written books on Keynesian economics. My specific interest in the *General Theory* is as a student of investing. If you can glean some of Keynes's main points about economic ecology—the relationships between the various forces of capitalism—you can become a more informed investor (as he did).

What the *General Theory* Means to Investors

The *General Theory* is by no means a bible on investing. It doesn't lay out a method for picking stocks, bonds, or other investments, nor does it tell you the right time to enter or leave the market. As a text on macroeconomic theory, it doesn't even give you a solid formula for predicting or describing economic movements. But what it does especially well is give you insights into mass psychology through the kind of universal guidance that's still powerful advice for investors. If you want a pure, classic approach to investing, though, the go-to book is still Benjamin Graham's *The Intelligent Investor*.[6] Oddly enough, although both men were firming up their theories in the 1930s, Graham—who was also burned by the 1929 crash—doesn't mention Keynes in his book, although Graham's student Warren Buffett plays a prominent role (he wrote the introduction and contributed an article to the appendix of Graham's book). While it's not known whether Keynes ever talked with Graham, they probably had some influence on each other, although perhaps not directly.

Keynes lays the groundwork for how to approach market psychology in the *General Theory*. As he discovered from his speculative activities in the 1920s, Keynes couldn't beat the market with a broad-based monetary theory. He abandoned the idea of using his theoretical knowledge to predict market cycles sometime in the early 1930s. The market always seemed to know something he didn't. Here are some of his key insights:

- **There is no automatic economic reset.** The conventional wisdom before the *General Theory* rested on Say's law, which posited that supply automatically creates its own demand. When market downturns occurred, capitalism would automatically self-correct, and demand for goods and services would return fairly quickly. Keynes found that notion outdated and, in the case of the 1930s, incredibly inaccurate. Investors can't always expect that a bear market will instantly revert to a bull market. The economy is sometimes painfully slow to recover.
- **Lack of demand translates into unemployment.** Another shibboleth of classical economics maintained that when downturns occurred, wages would drop, leading employers to hire more people. Keynes argued that when people were unemployed and were saving rather than consuming,

aggregate demand for goods and services would decline. When employment was increased (by any means), demand would return. In other words, someone who is out of work will not be buying things and supporting businesses that produce consumer goods. When the overall economy is limping along you want to use any means possible to increase employment. More workers mean more sales and more taxes, and this can refloat a sinking economy.

♦ **Money supply isn't always an effective fulcrum.** Increasing the money supply and lowering interest rates did not trigger a sustainable rebound in the 1930s (and has produced a poor recovery from 2009 to 2012). It doesn't always provide enough of an incentive for businesses to hire and turn the unemployed back into consumers again. Government intervention to create employment is often warranted to jump-start the economy. That's why the New Deal programs were enacted. The private sector wasn't responding to low interest rates; it was still laying workers off. The public sector had to fix what Keynes called "magneto trouble"; that is, it had to provide some kind of jump start to reignite consumer demand.

♦ **When people are employed, this has a confidence multiplier effect.** Keynes didn't provide an explicit formula for how this worked (although his follower John Hicks did in 1937), but it's simple.[7] When people are employed, they buy goods and services. When companies that provide those things see demand increasing, they hire more workers, who, in turn, consume more. This starts a virtuous cycle that leads to economic growth. In a nutshell, you can't have a robust consumer-based economy without strong employment creation. Investors need to see that companies are producing decent bottom lines. For that to happen, they need to have customers who can afford to buy their goods and services.

◆ **When people do not have confidence in the economy, they save.** This is a fairly consistent trait of mass economic behavior. Keynes found that people have a *marginal propensity to consume*. They are likely to save more when the economy is sour and spend more when things look brighter. When income increases, they spend a fraction of their earnings.[8] While savings is generally a good thing, too much savings reduces overall demand. Keynes wanted to shift the balance to get the majority of the population spending again. Investors can readily see when there's too much saving rather than spending. It's reflected in retail sales, wholesale prices, and inventories. Companies with declining sales and earnings are rarely good investments.

◆ **There are irrational elements behind the economy and markets.** Any discipline that claims to be a science, at least in the post-Enlightenment view, must be able to measure things. However, Keynes found that "animal spirits" were beyond economists' measuring tools and could have powerful impacts on the economy (much more on this in the next chapter). Consumer and investor confidence plays a large, often unmeasurable part of this equation. If investors *en masse* don't feel confident that the economy can support share prices or lead to growth in earnings, they will depress the market. The opposite is true during boom times.

◆ **The paradox of thrift can impede economic growth.** Although saving is generally seen as a virtuous activity, when everybody is saving (and not investing or spending) during economic downturns, the money that they are saving is not flowing back into the economy—hence the *paradox of thrift*. People may *want* to be liquid and have the ability to get their hands on cash to pay their bills, endure a jobless stretch, or cover emergencies. As John Kenneth Galbraith explains in

Economics in Perspective, "There is no assurance, as the classical economists held, that, because of lowered interest rates, these savings will be invested, which is to say, spent. They may be held unspent for a variety of precautionary reasons that reflect the individual or firm's need or wish for liquid assets— again, in Keynes's term, his, her or its liquidity preference."[9]

For practicing Keynesians such as Nobel Prize–winning economist Paul Krugman, the *General Theory* was nothing less than "an epic journey out of the intellectual darkness."[10] As a result of Keynes's broadside challenge to classical economics, "suddenly the idea that mass unemployment is the result of inadequate demand, long a fringe heresy, became completely comprehensible, indeed obvious."[11] Outside of the academic sphere, Krugman notes, the *General Theory* still ignites ideas on how to revive economic activity:

> Over the past 70 years, *The General Theory* has shaped the views even of those who haven't heard of it, or believe they disagree with it. . . . Even self-proclaimed supply-side economists, who claim to have refuted Keynes, fall back on unmistakably Keynesian stories to explain why the economy turned down in a given year.[12]

The grand umbrella of Keynesian stimulus shielded even those who espoused hostility to government intervention during economic troughs. One week after the attacks of September 11, 2001, President George W. Bush asked Americans for their "continued participation and confidence in the American economy."[13] Bush's "go out and spend" exhortation didn't trigger the full economic recovery the country was hoping for after the 9/11 attacks, nor did a similar plea inspire frenetic consumerism in 2008–2009 in the wake of the most catastrophic financial debacle since the 1930s. Nevertheless, it was a clear *Keynesian* plea to step up aggregate demand for consumer goods. That's a clarion call that still moves the business cycle, which is an essential element for any investor to watch.

As Graham, Buffett, and others had discovered long before 2001, in practice, the animal spirits that were depressing markets—and consumer demand—would also make securities prices more attractive. One could buy more shares of well-managed companies at a lower cost. Then, when the business cycle turned around, those investments would show appreciation. This is called "buy low and hold."

The *General Theory*'s Insights for Investors

While the *General Theory* isn't as useful to investors as Graham and Dodd's *Security Analysis* (Keynes doesn't provide any formulas for selecting investments), Keynes lays some important groundwork for fundamental investing and behavioral analysis. There's a gold mine in Chapter 12 of the *General Theory*. Here are some of the highlights:

1. **It's not the blind forecast of a company's expectations that matters, but the confidence we place in it.** Keynes places a value "on the likelihood of our best forecast turning out quite wrong."[14] So it follows that if the consensus Wall Street forecast indicates a certain range of earnings per share, what are the chances that a company will beat or underperform that forecast? What are the chances that something will go wrong?

2. **What is the company's book value?** This is a core principle of value investing that tries to determine what a company

would be worth to shareholders if all its assets were liquidated.[15] The difference between the book value and the current market value (the share price) shows either a premium or
a discount. Most value investors prefer to buy at a discount,
believing that the market will probably price the stock higher
at a later date. "There is no sense in building up a new enterprise at a cost greater than that at which a similar existing
enterprise can be purchased . . . thus certain classes of investment are governed by the average expectation of those who
deal on the Stock Exchange as revealed in the price of shares,
rather than by the genuine expectations of the professional
entrepreneur."[16] Although the efficient market theory was
more than 30 years in the future when Keynes wrote this, I
suspect that he wouldn't agree that the market prices every
stock efficiently. There are some mispricings that investors
can exploit.

3. **The market doesn't know everything.** Again, as a refu-
   tation of the belief that the free market prices every asset
   correctly, Keynes knew that mass ignorance can contribute
   to mispricing: "The element of real knowledge in the valuation of investments by those who own them has seriously
   declined."[17]

4. **The market can be irrational and produce noise.** Short-
   term news and results often should have little impact on
   prices, but they may be seen as part of a trend. "Day-to-day
   fluctuations in the profits of existing investments . . . tend to
   have an altogether excessive, and even an absurd, influence
   on the market."[18]

5. **The market can change faster than you can change your
   mind.** It doesn't take much to move a stock price quickly.
   When the herd moves, it may not be in the right direction. "A conventional valuation which is established as the

outcome of the mass psychology of a larger number of ignorant individuals is liable to change violently as the result of a sudden fluctuation of opinion due to factors which do not really make much difference to prospective yield; since there will be no strong roots of conviction to hold it steady."[19] Prices change at the speed of light, sometimes based only on rumors or on high-frequency trading errors.

6. **Short-term thinking increases volatility.** Liquidity isn't always a good thing. Keynes bemoaned the market's similarity to games like Snap, Old Maid, and Musical Chairs, and even to a beauty contest. Under this view, market participants are trying to guess "what the average opinion expects average opinion to be."[20] So investors end up employing the same groupthink and chasing the same "beautiful" stocks, but individual skepticism should be highly prized. "The social object of skilled investment should be to defeat the dark forces of time and ignorance which envelop our future."[21]

7. **It pays to be a contrarian.** Keynes, as you may have noted, didn't have much patience with short-term traders who followed the crowd, even though during the 1920s he was a fast-and-loose speculator. In the *General Theory*, he lauds the "long-term investor, he who promotes the public interest, who will come in for the most criticism. . . . For it is in the essence of his behavior that he should be eccentric, unconventional and rash in the eyes of average opinion."[22] Keynes certainly raised a few eyebrows in his management of King's College's and two insurance companies' funds. By the end of the 1930s, though, his rashness had paid off.

8. **There's a difference between speculation and investment.** Building upon his growing disdain for short-term traders, Keynes called *speculation* "the activity of forecasting the psychology of the market."[23] In contrast, *enterprise* forecasts the

prospective "yield of assets over their whole life."[24] In this one short phrase, he basically lays the cornerstone for the school of value investors: they look at a company's fundamental valuation over the long term and ignore the short-term noise. When the long-term view is imperiled, Keynes presciently states, is "when the enterprise becomes the bubble on a whirlpool of speculation."[25] Even good stocks can become overvalued in a market dominated by a mania, as Keynes witnessed in 1928 and most of us saw in 2000 and 2007.

9. **Fundamental analysis matters, but it's not enough.** We can easily calculate book values and probabilities and determine which companies are probably bargains relative to their market price. But we can't escape the linchpin of Keynes's worldview on markets: *animal spirits.* "This means, unfortunately, not only that slumps and depressions are exaggerated in degree, but that economic prosperity is excessively dependent upon a political and social atmosphere which is congenial to the average business man."[26] If businesses don't have confidence in the current economy, they won't invest or hire. Mass emotions still rule.

10. **Don't cling blindly to conventional wisdom.** Keynes's final words in his masterpiece echo his distrust of his own adopted profession. "Practical men, who believe themselves to be quite exempt from any intellectual influences, are usually the slaves of some defunct economist. Madmen in authority, who hear voices in the air, are distilling their frenzy from some academic scribbler of a few years back."[27]

Keynes's lively prose in the midst of an otherwise stolid treatise on economics still calls to us. Chapter 12 of the *General Theory*, from which all of these quotes are taken, came not from Keynes's theoretical musings, but from his practical experience as an investor. He was like St. Augustine, having discovered a deep, inner faith after renouncing the libertine ways of speculation that had driven him in the 1920s. He was wary of the crowd, ready to ride an old, steady mule rather than jumping back on a thoroughbred. This is Keynes for the ages, showing us what drives the economy and employment while telling us how *not* to invest. This one chapter is an advice book by itself, and it stands the test of time in its emphasis on fundamental principles and its nod to behavioral factors beyond our control.

Keynes Collapses

Fighting an economic war on two fronts in the political and investment arenas, Keynes was thoroughly depleted as the decade came to a close. Nevertheless, he was a durable cheerleader for stimulating demand. As he was writing his *General Theory*, he was also talking on the radio, trying to charm his country into stimulating economic demand:

> Therefore, O patriotic housewives, sally out tomorrow early into the streets and go to the wonderful sales which are everywhere advertised. You will do yourselves good—for never were things so cheap, cheap beyond your dreams.[28]

In fact, Keynes was trying to dissuade the British public from *practicing* his paradox of thrift. In the public policy sphere, Keynes pushed his ideas for government investment in a loan-financed public works program through his *London Times* series entitled "The Means to Prosperity," which appeared in March 1933.[29] Despite his vigorous efforts to promote his job creation plan, Keynes failed to see much progress, even after he gained a brief audience with FDR. He was frustrated and "had come to see that there was no magic formula that would easily guarantee recovery,"[30] according to Roger Backhouse and Bradley Bateman, who have written extensively on Keynes's place in history.

Even though his *General Theory* began a revolution by suggesting that unemployment surges during downturns didn't need to be severe, economist Hyman Minsky found that the view of Keynes's book "is that no such tendency to achieve and then sustain full employment exists; that is, the basic path of a capitalist economy is cyclical."[31]

A year after Keynes published the *General Theory*, his heart gave out. The economist had never been in robust health, but heart disease—believed to have been caused by a bacterial infection of his heart muscle—felled him in the spring of 1937. The man who had at least four extraordinary simultaneous careers was knocked flat by chest pains and breathlessness. He retreated to his bed and later to a Welsh sanitarium to convalesce, attended by the ever-devoted Lydia. He had felt something go awry as early as 1931, when challenges in the world economy and his portfolio had forced him to radically change his worldview. Now he was a virtual invalid. The doctors could do little for him at the time other than tell him to relax and cut back on his insane schedule.

Nevertheless, his investment management work had already moved boldly in a different direction. Money management had become infinitely less stressful than his speculative plunging in the 1920s and early 1930s. Having established a value bias in his investing in the 1930s, and being aware that animal spirits were creating mischief in the markets, he was armed with some powerful insights that would make him a better investor. His observations on the irrational nature of market behavior could be better measured by future economists: there was enormous untapped value for investors who truly could divine Keynes's animal spirits.

KEYNESIAN KEYSTONES

Prospective Yield

When Keynes tossed overboard the prevailing wisdom of the time that markets would somehow correct themselves after a downturn, he became a heretic in many ways. He was asserting that markets *can't* have perfect knowledge, nor can they correct the faults of rampant speculation and overzealous lending. Emotions can rule us and compel us to make short-term decisions based on sentiment rather than intellect. There are better ways to invest if we seek high-quality investment at a good price. But to maintain this discipline, we may have to act like Ulysses and plug our ears with wax as we try to avoid the sirens in the media. We should abandon the casino mentality of Wall Street. What happens on a daily basis doesn't matter. We need to stay focused on what Keynes called "prospective yield," or the prospect of future earnings and dividends. We can't know the future, but if a company's financial outlook is reasonably certain, that's what we should focus on, or we'll be misled by the animal spirits that dominate the market.

How can we defy the underlying emotion or confidence of the market? It's not easy to buy when others are selling. You need to reframe this as taking advantage of opportunities. Sometimes animal spirits lead the market to shift too much in one direction or the other. Markets can be overbought and oversold. It's when pessimism rules that the best prices can be found, but investment selection always depends on the companies you're buying. As I noted in the previous chapter, you still have to pay attention to the intrinsic fundamentals that were important to Keynes—long-term earnings growth, dividends, and enterprise value—and invest accordingly.

6

Animal Spirits: The Birth of Behavioral Investing

"Worldly wisdom teaches that it is better for reputation to fail conventionally than to succeed unconventionally." The profound wisdom of Keynes's statement reaches into every nook and cranny of the investment world. Slavishly following conventional wisdom proves unwise, as the frequently trod path often leads to disappointment.

—DAVID SWENSEN[1]

AS KEYNES'S CHEST ACHED MIGHTILY AND HE STRUGGLED FOR breath, the stock market suffered a myocardial infarction of its own. In the worst nosedive since 1929–1931 (and the second-worst in the century), the market gave up nearly 40 percent of its value in 1937. Keynes, who was being nursed by his mother and Lydia in Cambridge, was driven to an upper-class sanatorium in Wales. Since this was long before pacemakers, bypass surgery, and statin drugs, all the doctors could do was recommend copious amounts of bed rest away from his familiar environment and his ever-pressing schedule of advising, writing, lecturing, and managing money. They promised him a recovery within six months, although Keynes would never again have the Promethean energy that had relentlessly driven him. All of his portfolios seemed to track his debilitated state.

Although he managed to relay investment directions to his brilliant colleague Richard Kahn, the two insurance company portfolios, King's College's funds, and his own personal account were hammered. By this time, Keynes was a fervent believer in *holding* stocks and had loaded up all of the portfolios under his aegis with his "pets." Having faith in his selections, he refused to sell in a falling market, with the declines coming in waves throughout the year. He quietly watched as he lost two-thirds of his wealth; his net assets plummeted from £506,222 at the end of 1936 to £181,244 by the end of 1938, Skidelsky found.[2] His gross income fell by two-thirds.[3] Along with his personal paper losses, Keynes had to answer to King's College and the two insurance companies whose funds he managed, National Mutual and Provincial. Their boards were irate.

While National Mutual accepted Keynes's resignation after the 1937 decline, he managed to convince the directors at Provincial and at King's that his approach was still solid. He wasn't afraid of staying in his positions while the market went the other way. By defying the animal spirits that were taking the market south, he wanted to avoid giving in to fear and dumping stocks that he thought would be sound in the long run. Keynes braced for the inevitable criticism, but he was aware that this was the sort of time when disciplined investors proved their mettle. Money manager Martin Conrad would later observe that Keynes "emphasized that individual investment profits are largely determined by how investors behave at market tops and bottoms—which is where price volatility concentrates, where sudden spikes occur, where the big investment mistakes are made."[4]

Why buck the trend when everyone else was selling? Why sit on losses when it would have been easier to bail? Ever dwelling on the perennial issue of *uncertainty*, Keynes retreated to what he knew and tried to distance himself from the market's short-term calamity. What did he know that would be valid in the future? He had faith in his companies; his *pets* would outlast the slump and prosper when the economy turned around. They had *value* that would not be vanquished by the wild animal spirits of pure panic. Sooner or later, confidence would be restored and others would see the value in his stocks. Throughout most of the 1930s, restoration of widespread *confidence* was the essential element that was missing from the despair-ridden decade. At every turn, he saw confidence as a core element of positive animal spirits: bankers would lend again; businesses would invest and hire; people would get back to work and spend money.

This powerful theme would be revisited in the wake of the 2008 meltdown. What would it take to stimulate the economy after the credit bubble burst and housing collapsed? Clearly the private sector was scared and was unwilling to hire or spend money. After all, trillions of dollars of financial and housing wealth had evaporated, some six million people had lost their jobs, and it would take years for a firm recovery to take hold. While the stock market started on a bullish path that began in mid-2009, the rest of the economy didn't really follow that script, and economists like Paul Krugman declared that the economy was in its own kind of depression. Once again, scholars and pundits turned to Keynes to examine what he had said in the 1930s on the subject of the erosion of popular confidence. When he was asked to lecture at the University of Chicago in 1931, he told his audience that the first line of approach in conquering the malaise of the Depression was the "restoration of confidence both to the lender and to the borrower."[5] Keynes, who later explored this in more depth in his *General Theory of Employment, Interest and Money*, observed that widespread pessimism created a "vicious circle" that shut down normal business activity and consumer spending.

While he advocated extensive government public works programs to generate jobs, income, and consumption (a policy that was later incorporated into Franklin Delano Roosevelt's many make-work programs), Keynes was deeply concerned that "the shock to confidence" could not be overcome by the "vague expectations or hopes of the business world."[6] Yet Keynes went further into the little-studied realm of mass psychology and decision management, as we've seen in the previous chapter. He wanted to know how this juggernaut of opinion, fear, despair, and dynamic tension could be described in a more scientific sense. His economics sought to understand and measure mass emotion.

PORTFOLIO NARRATIVE

National Mutual Life Assurance Society

Keynes wasn't always in sync with the directors of the funds he managed or with his longtime partner Oswald Falk. As he became more convinced that animal spirits were wreaking havoc upon the markets, he became less convinced that he could track and make money from commodity or credit cycles. His confidence, intellectual rigor, and steadfast nature didn't entirely sway F. N. Curzon, the acting chairman of National Mutual. Keynes managed the insurance company's funds from 1921 through October 1938, when he resigned (he was also recuperating from his heart attack at the time and had cut back on his money management duties). When Keynes became a celebrity in London financial circles in the 1920s, his annual speeches to the National Mutual board were celebrated events. Several of them are included in Volume 12 of Keynes's *Collected Writings* and other books. In his speeches, Keynes explained what he thought was happening in the markets that year and discussed some of his strategies. Here are some condensed passages from letters and speeches that sample the highlights of his tenure leading up to the crash of 1929 and into the 1930s:

1921   Keynes and Falk discuss the use of an "industrial index" that tracks major stocks in key industries such as mining (Rio Tinto) and manufacturing (Associated Portland Cement).

The portfolio is dominated by British and foreign government securities, reflecting the conservative nature of the institutional portfolios of the time.

1925   Falk is "not prophesying crash like that of 1921 . . . crash should be easily avoided."

1927   Keynes writes, "It's a dangerous market . . . the fall of agricultural prices is important . . . the balance of probability is in favor of lower interest rates than before the war [World War I]."

1928   "I'm cautious and unwilling to be overinvested. . . . Is there inflation in the U.S.? I predict that stocks won't slump severely."

1929   Falk writes on June 28: "It's a good moment for making carefully selected purchases." Keynes replies on July 2 that "the market seems to me to be a dangerous one relative to the prospects of larger further gains."

Source: King's College Archives and *The Collected Writings of John Maynard Keynes*, ed. Donald Moggridge (London: Macmillan, 1971–1989), Vol. 12.

The Sweet Science of Animal Spirits

Keynes's recognition of mass psychology sowed the seeds of what would later become known as *behavioral economics*. Pioneered by Daniel Kahneman, Amos Tversky, Richard Thaler, and others in the 1980s, it embraced Keynes's idea and transformed it into experimental science. Kahneman, a psychologist, later won a Nobel Prize for his pioneering work. Economist Marcello De Cecco calls the *General Theory* "the foundation of modern behavioral finance."[7]

> By the time the turbulent decades of the 1920s and 1930s had passed, Keynes had changed his views in favor of what we now call behavioral finance. Rational agents may be present in forces to mount strategies against "noise traders," but their actions may not lead them to make profits and at the same time stabilize markets.[8]

Perhaps aided by the work of Freud and Jung, which was gaining popularity in the 1920s and 1930s, Keynes's observations on economic behavior, even if they didn't break any empirical new ground, created an intellectual edifice for future behavioral economists. "Conventions, representation and framing are concepts that recur all the time in Keynesian prose," De Cecco adds, "especially so in his most famous book [the *General Theory*], although the mixture of experimental psychology and probability theory that prevails in Kahneman and Tversky's works is also very similar to that used by Keynes in his *Treatise on Probability*."[9]

Keynes was also an inspiration to Robert Shiller, a Yale economics professor and pioneer in behavioral investing, and George Akerlof, who was teaching economics at the University of California–Berkeley. Akerlof's work on asymmetric market information and its impact on economic behavior won him the Nobel Prize in Economics.[10] Shiller's classic, *Irrational Exuberance* (Princeton, NJ: Princeton Press, 2005), provided a scintillating overview of the dot-com bubble and (later in the second edition) a framework for explaining the 2008 housing meltdown. Working together after the 2008 debacle, Akerlof and Shiller produced *Animal Spirits: How Human Psychology Drives the Economy, and Why It Matters for Global Capitalism*. Writing in the *Financial Times,* Clive Crook said that Akerlof and Shiller "argue that the key is to recover Keynes's insight about 'animal spirits'—the attitudes and ideas that guide economic action. The orthodoxy needs to be rebuilt, and bringing these psychological factors into the core of economics is the way to do it."[11]

The school of behavioral economics was fueled by Keynes's insights into market behavior in Chapter 12 in the *General Theory*. Although modern economists and social psychologists didn't take up Keynes's challenge to *measure* emotional behavior in economic terms until nearly half a century later, the same questions that Keynes faced in the 1930s still perplex us today: Why do manias, bubbles, and panics still occur in a globalized, information-centric world? What triggers them? How can we avoid them in the future? Perched on the pedestal of the *General Theory*, Akerlof and Shiller were asking these questions in 2009 as the global economy reeled from the credit, mortgage, and banking meltdown of 2008.

According to Akerlof and Shiller, *animal spirits*, thanks to Keynes, has become an "economic term, referring to a restless and inconsistent element in the economy. It refers to our peculiar relationship with ambiguity or uncertainty. Sometimes we are paralyzed by it. Yet at other times it refreshes or energizes us, overcoming our fears and indecisions."[12]

Like Keynes, Akerlof and Shiller claim that modern economics can't precisely measure or track the mood swings that sway markets and trigger changes in economic cycles. But they can't deny the power of these mood swings, which can "change the social fabric, our level of trust in one another and our willingness to undertake effort and engage in self sacrifice."[13] The authors, who had been studying markets for decades prior to writing the book, were viewing animal spirits through the lens of the 2008 debacle, which not only ignited a brutal recession in housing, financial services, and other areas, but pared more than six million jobs, brought down two major Wall Street firms (Bear Stearns and Lehman Brothers), and created financial havoc for other countries from Greece to Iceland.

The financial bubble, which was based on cheap credit and securitized, virtually unregulated trading, was also buoyed by a universal sense of confidence, Akerlof and Shiller maintain. No one in recent memory had experienced a major drop in real estate prices, nor could anyone conceive of supply outstripping demand in both the credit and the housing markets. The massive destruction of wealth and employment in Keynes's time had been nearly erased from the collective cultural memory of North America and Europe. Rather than hewing to theory, Akerlof and Shiller proposed that economists monitor behavior in the economy that can be observed. Here is their neo-Keynesian framework for describing the role of animal spirits:

♦ **Confidence is the cornerstone.** Akerlof and Shiller maintain that our perception of confidence in the economy creates feedback loops that "amplify disturbances."[14] Is your brother-in-law buying a home with the intention of "flipping it" to make a quick profit? Did the market go up again today? Isn't it time to invest "before it's too late"? It's a good time to invest because the market can *always* go higher. These are common emotions during a confidence phase, as Shiller noted in *Irrational Exuberance* and tracked through ongoing focus groups. Like pessimism, widespread confidence has its own multiplier effect that propels bull markets and excessive speculation. Today, well-known surveys such as the Conference Board reports and the Michigan Consumer Sentiment Index attempt to measure confidence, which often leads to increased consumer spending and economic activity. In contrast, low confidence "has caused credit markets to freeze,"[15] an event that happened in the wake of the Lehman Brothers collapse in late 2008.

♦ **Fairness, corruption, and scandals.** Emotional reactions to these events often trigger crises of confidence. Akerlof and Shiller trace three economic downturns to various scandals. The most recent—and most severe—was the housing and credit meltdown that started to rear its ugly head in 2007 and culminated in the crash of 2008.[16] It wasn't fair that Wall Street bankers who had made billions from derivatives trades and securitization of mortgages largely escaped jail time with some of their fortunes intact. And clearly much was amiss with the credit ratings process that gave AAA ratings to inferior subprime loans and led to a foreclosure crisis (this is the subject of an ongoing federal lawsuit as this goes to press). When there's collusion in manipulating the markets, the picture that the investing public sees is asymmetrical; that is, insiders have different information that benefits them at the expense of others. In the public's view, bankers became the Gatsbys of Keynes's era. Financial predation and exploitation were the hidden rules of the game.

♦ **Average investors are deceived.** When asset prices are rising, it's often the result of bubble-fueled speculation or inflation. Wages can also fail to keep up with actual increases in consumer prices. The economist Irving Fisher, in his 1928 book

The Money Illusion, lays out a case for how the deception works. A worker may think that his modest raise is keeping up with the cost of living, but in terms of "real" inflation-adjusted dollars, he is falling behind. "Even our hero, John Maynard Keynes, explained income distribution for economies at full employment by assuming the workers fail to negotiate increases in wages to offset inflation," Akerlof and Shiller note.[17]

So how do animal sprits take shape as an economic catalyst? Why did the stock market rise fivefold between 1920 and 1929 and then lose all of its gains between 1929 and 1932? What about the great bull market after World War II, which lasted from 1954 to 1973, only to lose half of its value in the following *year*? Akerlof and Shiller argue that no economist has ever succeeded in explaining these gyrations, which are not explained by "changes in interest rates, subsequent dividends or earnings or by anything else."[18] They point to a leverage, feedback, and leverage cycle. Lenders feel confident, so they lend freely. Everyone sees asset prices climbing, so lending increases. When the loop is disrupted, lending contracts—along with prices.[19]

The same thing happens in the stock market. Confidence rebounds after a slump, and investors start bidding up stock prices. Those who were saving their money see that they can double their returns in the stock market, so they buy stocks as well. The feedback of higher stock prices convinces them that their *confidence* is justified, and that lowers their *perception* of risk, when in fact the actual risk of loss hasn't changed at all—and in many cases is much higher due to inflated valuations. There's a reason why animal spirits are personified by bulls and bears. They are bipolar and unpredictable, yet highly observable. Shiller's real estate focus groups, for example, tracked the *dominant narrative* of these cycles. Are investors confident enough to buy? What are they seeing? How do they describe their attitude? While this is hardly an exact science, the prevailing narrative is an indicator in itself.

In attempting to understand the prevailing narrative of animal spirits, Shiller regularly looks for "contagion, social epidemics and memes."[20] These are social messages that describe the narrative. Are stock investment clubs booming? Are grandmothers investing in tech companies they don't understand? Does a company engender a horde of cultlike followers? Are ordinary homeowners buying homes to flip them? Ultimately, though, you have to accept the fact that animal spirits are quirky, unreliable, and difficult to forecast—much like capitalism itself. You need to keep a close eye on the tenor of the times, which often runs from mania to melancholy.

> Capitalism fills the supermarkets with thousands of items that meet our fancy. But if our fancy is for snake oil, it will produce that, too. . . . Yes, capitalism is good. But yes, it also has its excesses. And it must be watched.[21]

Animal Spirits and Market Inefficiency

In a rational economic world, the market would price everything from a pair of shoes to Apple stock fairly based on its intrinsic merits and supply and demand. Stock prices would accurately reflect future earnings, cash flow, dividend yield, and enterprise prospects. Most of the time, the market does this fairly well. But then, like Loki the trickster, the gremlins of animal spirits come to make mischief. Companies with back-of-the-napkin business plans fetched wild initial public offering prices. Single-family ranch houses garnered stratospheric price gains. The rational market then does its reckoning, and prices crash. This has been the way of the world since markets came about.

According to behavioral economists Hersh Shefrin and Meir Statman at Santa Clara University, investors may not be rational, but they certainly are *normal*; they follow certain persistent behavioral patterns that lead them astray. Nodding to the work of Keynes, the economists note that "securities prices often diverge from their intrinsic values."[22] They cite Hyman Minsky, a leading Keynes interpreter, who pointed to the fact that "financial innovation can create economic euphoria for a while before destabilizing the economy and hurling it into crises rivaling the Great Depression."[23]

Also writing in the wake of the 2008 meltdown, Shefrin and Statman developed a behavioral investing model that takes into account "equal wealth-weighted averages of investors' subjective valuations." Like Shiller, they are focusing on what investors think is going on, not on rational economic models.

Although a bevy of tools for creating risk-adjusted portfolios has certainly evolved over the years, if the models created ignore the power of animal spirits, they will not adequately incorporate the potential for a destructive "black swan" event like those of 1929, 1937, 1987, or 2008. Yet we need to recognize the kinds of behavioral buzzards that can gnaw away at our psyches when it comes to investing.

A VOODOO DEFINITION OF ANIMAL SPRITS

In a recent visit to New Orleans, I reframed animal spirits as an intangible form of mass human emotion. It can't be explicitly measured, but it's always within the part of our nature that acts quickly out of fear, compulsion, and survival. Voodoo priestesses call it "juju" or "mojo." It's the impulse that drives us to drive a little faster, drink too much, and perhaps buy that stock that has a certain cachet.

Money manager Lee Munson, in his book *Rigged Money*, calls animal spirits: "The mojo, baby. It's reality, nature, and the primal state of it all things. When you graduate from college and you have to start paying your student loans, you start to feel the animal spirits. It's the thing that gets you up in the morning—gut instinct. It's not rational, it's right. Animal spirits describes the madness of crowds and the irrational behavior of people. It accurately explains why some people make money and some people are born losers. It's the difference between Hegel and Nietzsche. Nietzsche won."[24]

Daniel Kahneman and Amos Tversky (and their behavioral economic acolytes) caged Keynes's animal spirits in a series of experiments to determine what people actually did when they were making monetary and other life decisions. They discovered a number of roadblocks that impede our success:

- **Overconfidence bias.** At some point in our lives, most of us are like Keynes in the 1920s: we think that we have a global view and that we know more than we actually know. Kahneman and Tversky measured the extent to which people were overconfident, and it spanned every area of life. The people they observed consistently thought that they were smarter, better money managers, and better drivers, for example, than the "average" person. We see overconfidence all the time in personal money management. Those who trade securities more than average consistently earn lower-than-average returns. In fact, they rarely earn more than their trading commissions, according to a famous study by Professors Brad Barber and

Terrance Odean, who did their research at the University of California.[25]

♦ **Excessive optimism.** We think bull markets will last forever, so we buy at the top of the market, when prices are high and the downside risk is great. We tend to underestimate risk. Kahneman details this trait in a number of examples in his classic, *Thinking, Fast and Slow*.[26] Consumed with optimism and confidence, we then become "underinsured against extreme and unlikely possibilities."[27] Even Keynes, who thought his extensive research and genius for macroeconomic theory gave him the upper hand, was convinced that he had an advantage. No one does when it comes to timing the market unless you have inside knowledge or are simply lucky.

♦ **Framing errors.** We see decisions through a narrow lens. A stock price is too low because we *feel* that it is. There's little rational basis for this kind of thinking, and it gets us into trouble.

♦ **Anchoring.** We'll hold on to a certain position at a certain price, even though it makes no sense. Have you ever kept a losing stock because you're anchored to the price you paid for it? I certainly have. It *must* bounce back! The rational thing to do is to sell losers and take a tax loss. But few people want to cut loose from that anchor. We generally obey the main tenet of Kahneman and Tversky's "prospect theory," which holds that losses and regret are much more painful than gains, so we avoid triggering a loss.

♦ **Mental accounting.** We tend to put things in cerebral buckets that constrain decision making. That speculative stock we bought is in the "mad money" account, so we can avoid dealing with its drop in value.

Many, if not all, of these errors can be avoided by taking a balanced, thoughtful approach to risk and probability, which

Kahneman told me is the "slow process" of cognition that takes time. Our reptilian brain, which is nimble and impulsive and hates loss, tells us to pull the trigger on buying while putting the brakes on selling. We need to stop, step back, think about our decisions more carefully, and employ Keynes's view of probability: What are the degrees of certainty behind an investment decision? What's the downside? Will the contemplated purchase make sense (in terms of appreciation, dividends, or liquidity) years from now? We can't go on making decisions from moment to moment. We need to take the time to reflect, to learn, and to decide.

When we slow down to take our time and use our analytical abilities to make a sound decision—unhampered by skittish animal spirits—most of us can make better decisions and lead more prosperous lives. Only then can we step back and see our ultimate goal, what Keynes called (in 1937) "a decent level of consumption for everyone; and when that is high enough, toward the occupation of our energies in the non-economic interests of our lives."[28] Keynes was forced to slow down because of his damaged heart. But anybody who has a healthy mind and body can and *should* slow down in order to make better investment decisions. As we'll see in the next chapter, a more relaxed pace not only made Keynes a better investor, but allowed him to produce his best work.

A MODERN GAUGE FOR ANIMAL SPRITS

The CAPE

Shiller (along with John Campbell, a finance professor at Harvard) developed a "cyclically adjusted price-earnings ratio," or CAPE. It gives a relative historical gauge of investor sentiment about stock prices today, based on the average inflation-adjusted earnings from the previous 10 years. It's useful because it can compare current investor beliefs about what a dollar of earnings should be worth—the price/earnings ratio—to historical high-water marks. P/E ratios tend to be high in times of irrational exuberance and lower in less-confident times. Here are some peaks and valleys:

Date	CAPE
Black Tuesday (1929)	30
Black Monday (1987)	16
Dot-com peak (1999)	44
Mortgage meltdown (2008)	27
Median	15.87
Mean	16.46

When this metric starts to head north of its mean, then investors may be overbidding on stock prices. They are probably headed for a fall when the ratio heads above 25. While this is not a perfect meter of market sentiment, it's a useful comparative tool.

KEYNESIAN KEYSTONES

Spurning Animal Spirits

The ultimate defense against being bamboozled by animal spirits is being vigilant. Watching stock ratios such as price/earnings ratios for the S&P 500 and other indexes tells you something about investors who are willing to bid stocks ever higher—or lower. Do the fundamentals of a company justify the increases in its stock price? If not, it could be due for a fall. Look at historical price/earnings ratios compared to today's p/e's. Also pay attention to the popular narrative. Every time you hear "this time is different" during a market rally, guard your nest egg closely. Remember that animal spirits are the soul of volatility, which never goes away. If you can't take the risk of being overwhelmed by the negative force of animal spirits, you need a healthy portion of your portfolio in bonds, inflation-protected securities, and cash. Be careful with leverage, and don't follow the financial blather on cable channels. And if you're a long-term investor—and can handle market risk—then hold on to stocks with value and dividends, as Keynes did. You'll be rewarded when the mood swing shifts the market in your direction again.

Keynes's Pets

In general conversation I find people far too
depressed about our finances. The usual opinion
seems to be that the war will leave this country
seriously impoverished, and that we are heading
straight for inflation. After looking closely into the
real position, I feel much more buoyant than that.

—JOHN MAYNARD KEYNES, SEPTEMBER 23, 1940[1]

AFTER BEING TREATED WITH A DYE EXTRACT BY THE HUNGARIAN
doctor Janos Plesch, Keynes at first felt awful and could barely
stand. Then what would later be known as a sulfa antibiotic
effected a remarkable turnaround in the economist. Although it
was no lasting cure for his heart disease, he was able to take a
jaunt to Paris and take in the baths at Royat, near Vichy, with
Lydia.[2] Yet Keynes was not to enjoy much of a respite. Although
he thought at the time that Hitler was engaging in "more politics than war," the German dictator sent his troops into Poland
on September 1, 1939. Two days later, Britain declared war on

Germany. The British government didn't call upon Keynes immediately, although the economist knew he would eventually be
tapped by the Treasury Department to consult on war finances.[3]
His health, of course, was still an issue, although he was always
eager to serve in some capacity. By this time, his money management duties were somewhat lighter, as he had resigned from
National Mutual in 1938 after a dismal year and after clashing
with the board over his investment policy of sticking with his
"pet" stocks during a decline. He was no longer partnering with
Falk on any investment activities, as their relationship had soured
as well. Certain that Great Britain would need considerable financial resources to fight Hitler (especially from the wary Americans),
Keynes began to focus on ways to pay for the war.

The series of market train wrecks that had taken place in the
1930s had chastened Keynes. Perhaps he was no longer convinced that his macroeconomic theories could anticipate investor emotions on a large scale. There was too much *uncertainty*,
which always seemed to be dissonant with long-term expectations. Traders were too distracted to focus on the intrinsic value
of companies. Speculators were not serving the social purpose of
risk bearing, a view that he had held in the 1920s during his currency and commodity speculation. Now his guiding principle for
security selection was "faithfulness," that is, making solid selections and sticking with them. What was important now, as the
world went to war again, was long-term profitability. That meant
looking carefully at a company's enterprise. What did it do that
distinguished it from the competition over the long haul? How
could the company produce steady profits and dividends?

Keynes continued to firm up his investment philosophy and
was able to focus on maintaining his portfolios despite predictions that the war would ruin the economies of Britain and the
United States. When he regained his health, he was once again

able to juggle his myriad responsibilities as theatrical producer (the Arts Theatre), government advisor, speaker, writer, and portfolio manager. An efficient multitasker, "Keynes was incredibly quick at getting through his business and had huge powers of cutoff," Robert Skidelsky told me.[4] In addition to setting up programs to finance the war, Keynes had to fend off battles in the boardrooms of Provincial and National Mutual, which had suffered significant losses in the late 1930s.

Keynes himself had lost some 62 percent of his capital between 1936 and 1938 (he would never return to his high-water mark of 1936), which, in addition to his worries about the war, triggered spasms of anxiety.[5] Still, he maintained his policy over time, hewing closely to his new long-term investment method. When he died, his estate was worth some $36.5 million in 2013 dollars.[6] He also left a rare book and art collection worth £80,000, or more than $1.4 million today.[7] That's not exactly Bill Gates–or Warren Buffett–sized wealth, but it's astounding considering that his investing career spanned two world wars and the Great Depression.

Still, the idea of continuing to hold stocks when the world was entering its most catastrophic war probably seemed like lunacy to Keynes's fellow directors and investors. They challenged him and demanded that he defend his position in the face of long odds. Most level-headed managers would have retreated to government bonds, or even gold, in the face of the war's inflationary pressures. Barton Biggs, who writes in *Hedgehogging* that Keynes surpassed all of the "brilliant and bizarre characters in the hedge-fund world [circa 2006]," admired the economist for his fortitude:

> Even at the darkest moments in 1940 and 1941, Keynes was convinced that England and the United States would win and that the post-war world, if properly organized, would be

prosperous. If this didn't happen, it wouldn't make any difference whether an insurance company owned stock or not. When the chairman of National Mutual and its directors found this reasoning odd, he resigned in disgust.[8]

Even more incredibly, Keynes held on to his stock positions as London was being bombed and the American government (initially) expressed reluctance to join in another European war. Not only did he have confidence in his own stance, but he was utterly certain that the capitalist democracies would prevail and create a new world order after the war. I suspect that in 1940, like most of his contemporaries, Keynes had no idea what was ahead of England. The French army quickly collapsed, and the British expeditionary force at Dunkirk had to be evacuated. German U-boats had destroyed 1.5 million tons of British shipping by the autumn of that year. Nevertheless, Keynes marched into the war years holding his ground.

KEYNES'S VALUE-DRIVEN INVESTMENT POLICY

Institutional investors—and most wise individuals—need to have an *investment policy statement* before they start buying securities. This is a simple set of declarations concerning the purpose and composition of a portfolio. In Keynes's case, he was dedicated to taking dominant stock positions in companies that paid dividends and holding them for the long term. When the market tanked, he held fast to his policy. While his portfolios suffered paper losses in 1937–1938, they eventually bounced back. His focus on staying the course and maintaining his discipline proved profitable in the end. That's why you should craft a policy statement that's aligned with your appetite for risk. Fine-tune it once a year, and don't try to time the market.

Firm Principles for His Pets

Keynes had started honing his investment policy long before the war, having found ways to endure and bounce back from the market routs after 1929. In the wake of the disastrous 1937–1938 downturn, Keynes was called to account for the portfolio loss of £641,000 at National Mutual.[9] In a letter to National Mutual chairman F. N. Curzon (March 18, 1938), who had called him on the carpet for the loss and for refusing to liquidate his stock positions, Keynes replies feistily. Here are some of the highlights (using Keynes's numbered points):

1. I do not believe that selling at very low prices is a remedy for having failed to sell at high ones. . . . In my own case, I was of the opinion that the prices of sterling [British] securities were fully high in the spring. But I was prevented from taking advantage of this. . . . As soon as prices had fallen below a reasonable estimate of intrinsic value and long-period probabilities, there was nothing more to be done. It was too late to remedy any defects in previous policy, and the right course was to stand pretty well where one was.[10]

2. I feel no shame at being found owning a share when the bottom of the market comes. I do not think it is the business, far less the duty, of an institutional or any other serious investor to be constantly considering whether he should cut and run on a falling market, or to feel himself open to

blame if shares depreciate on his hands. . . . An investor is aiming, or should be aiming, primarily at long-period results, and should be solely judged by these. . . . The idea that we should all be selling out to the other fellow and should all be finding ourselves with nothing but cash at the bottom of the market is not merely fantastic, but destructive of the whole system.[11]

3. I do not agree that we have in fact done particularly badly. . . . Moreover, if our results are compared with those of the index, for a period, they are extremely good. We have done a great deal better than the index. . . . If we deal in equities; it is inevitable that there should be large fluctuations.[12]

Note that Keynes's courageous position is the opposite of what most portfolio managers would have done (and probably did) during the second-worst market price decline of the last 100 years. He held his positions because he still believed in his stocks. Was he being irrational or just bullheaded? It appears that Keynes was paying close attention to the intrinsic or book value of his holdings. He knew that they were worth *something* and that the market was rashly undervaluing them. Although it's not certain whether he added to these positions—buying more of his pets when they became bargains—he at least stuck with his investment policy of holding for long-term returns.

What Keynes did in 1937–1938 was atypical of most investors. He held firm to his principles and his idea of why the companies he had chosen deserved a place in his portfolios. This is an essential lesson for modern investors: if you think your companies have future potential, and you can ignore current market conditions, then hold onto them and buy more.

Keynes's Cambridge Pets

Two months later (in 1938), Keynes wrote a memo to the Estates Committee of King's College, reiterating his investment policy. The King's College portfolios had also posted large losses, so he wanted to reconnect with college officials concerning his original purpose and his current thinking. His ideas reflected the core of his philosophy in the 1930s, a mature view that not only presages behavioral economics, but shows its grounding in the value school of investing. Unlike at National, Keynes had free rein to manage money for the college.

After giving a brief summary of his rationale, Keynes defended his stay-put style, bemoaning that:

> the idea of wholesale shifts [selling stocks] is for various reasons impracticable and indeed undesirable. Most of those who attempt it sell too late and buy too late, and do both too often, incurring heavy expenses and developing too unsettled and speculative a state of mind, which, if it is widespread, has besides the grave social disadvantage of aggravating the scale of the fluctuations. I believe now that successful investment depends upon three principles:
>
> 1. A careful selection of a few investments (or a few types of investment) having regard to their cheapness in relation to their probable actual and potential intrinsic value over a period of years ahead and in relation to alternative investments at the time;
> 2. A steadfast holding of these in fairly large units through thick and thin, perhaps for several years, until they have fulfilled their promise or it is evident that they were purchased on a mistake;

3. A balanced investment position, i.e., a variety of risks in spite of individual holdings being large, and if possible *opposed* (italics mine) risks (e.g., a holding of gold shares amongst other equities, since they are likely to move in the opposite directions when there are general fluctuations).[13]

After laying out what would later become a manifesto for long-term, diversified investors, Keynes states another key rule: to avoid "second-class safe investments."[14] Although he doesn't elaborate on what those vehicles are, I'm assuming that he's referring to lower-rated (nongovernment) bonds. Ultimately, Keynes says that the "ideal investment portfolio is divided between the purchase of really secure future income (where future appreciation or depreciation will depend upon the rate of interest) and equities which one believes to be capable of a large improvement to offset the fairly numerous cases which, with the best skill in the world, will go wrong."[15]

If there's a more concise way of describing a long-term investment policy statement that maintains a balance between stocks and bonds, I don't know of it. After one of the most dreadful years in investing history, Keynes was giving us a workable template for all time. And he was far from finished with his groundbreaking work of managing other people's money, a job that for most people would have been nerve-racking and time-consuming, with enormous responsibilities and countless sleepless nights.

PORTFOLIO SNAPSHOT

King's College, Cambridge, Discretionary Portfolios

Since he faced little institutional resistance concerning *what* to buy and hold, Keynes had an unusual amount of freedom in managing money at Cambridge as first bursar. Although he was moving heavily into stocks in his other portfolios in the 1930s, Keynes had been buying stocks for King's College in the 1920s. Like his other purchases, they were timed to coincide with or anticipate commodity, credit, and business cycles. You'll notice that several of these stocks also appear in his other personal and institutional portfolios. Since he was also watching commodity prices, he bought companies that dealt in commodities, such as rubber, textile, and metals companies. Note his shift into the U.S. market in 1932, grabbing high-quality companies at great prices. Although it wasn't within the scope of this book to look at the King's College portfolio from Keynes's tenure to the present, if the college held onto positions like Siemens, General Electric, and Shell, with dividends reinvested, the gains would be impressive. Keynes's shift toward U.S. utilities appears to have been dividend-oriented. Even during the Depression, many of these companies paid out steady dividends that were as high as 7 percent, which was extraordinary in a deflationary time. He was also buying commodity contracts such as wheat and rubber during this time. Also note his repeat purchases of Austin, Leyland, and Hector Whaling, which were among his favorite pets. He was considerably less active during World War II, but his overall performance made King's one of the wealthiest colleges within Cambridge University, a status it enjoys today.

Here's a summary of his purchases over time:

1923 British American Tobacco, Bleachers Association, Brummer, Nobel, J&P Coats, Bradford Dyes, Fine Cotton Spinners, Crosses & Winkworth, India Rubber Gutta Percha, Siemens, Spillers, Platt Brothers, Maypole, Harden Colliers

1924	Swedish Matches, Bear Park Coal & Coke, Jute Industries, James Finlay, Shell, Burmak, Zinc Corp., Lakeview Investment Trust
1925	General Electric, Courtalds, Selabra Rubber, Siamese Tin, Malaysia Tin, Central Sumatra
1926	Great Western Railway, Southern Railway, Sudan, Burmah Oil, Southern Malaysia Tin, National Smelting, Rupp Tin, Leyland, Austin, Great Northern Telegraph
1928	P.R. Finance, Marconi, Wallpaper
1930	Hudson's Bay, Malaysia Tin, Southern Rail, Tri-Continental, San Paulo Coffee
1931	Shell, Leyland, Southern Railway, Imperial Chemical, Underground Electric, Austin, Dunlop Rubber
1930	Consolidated Gas of New York, General Motors, National Power & Light, Chrysler, B&O Railroad Commonwealth & Southern, Austin, Swedish Match, Malaysia Tin
1931	Johannesburg Consolidated, Union, El Oro, Hector Whaling
1932	United Gas, Commonwealth and Southern, Chicago & Rock Island RR, Austin
1933	Chrysler, Central States Electric, Austin
1934	American Cities Power, Canadian Hydro, Consolidated Diamonds, Homestake, Chicago Pneumatic Tool, Leyland, British Aeroplane, Hector Whaling
1935	Austin, Atlas, Hawker, Tri-Continental
1936	People's Gas, Austin, United Gas, Climax Molybdenum
1937	Leyland, Woolworth, Lancaster Cotton, GM, Lever, Austin
1946	Barclays, Richard Thomas & Baldwins

Source: Estates Committee reports, 1923–1946, King's College Archives.

Inside Keynes's Petting Zoo

There's little question that Keynes's investment style in the late 1930s was dynamic. Today we would call him a *tactical asset allocator*. Instead of assigning ironclad percentages to his allocation—say, 60 percent stocks and 40 percent bonds—he wanted to remain flexible. Tactical investors today also don't stick with a fixed allocation. They can reduce their holdings in stocks or bonds if there appears to be a shift in market conditions that might hurt those investments in the near term.

As he wrote F. C. Scott, chairman of Provincial (June 7, 1938), "the whole art is to vary the emphasis and the center of gravity of one's portfolio according to circumstances. Subject to a minimum in government securities and a maximum in ordinary shares [common stocks] I would strongly urge the desirability of the greatest possible flexibility."[16]

For Keynes in the late 1930s, "flexibility" meant allocating nearly 75 percent of his institutional portfolios to stocks and other non-government bond assets. As a concession, he wrote Scott that he was willing to raise the stake in British government bonds to as much as 40 percent.[17] On colonial government and foreign government securities, Keynes was clearly bearish, telling Scott, "I should be quite ready to cut them out altogether."[18] The remainder of the portfolio—from 20 to 30 percent—would be reserved for "different classes of ordinary shares."[19]

While Keynes adopted a concentrated approach of holding less than 100 stocks, he applied other screens to find his pets. He sought small- or mid-cap companies and high dividend payers, and he bought when some of his favorite companies fell in price. Gavyn Davies of Fulcrum Asset Management noted Keynes's discipline:

He became a contrarian investor, mainly buying stocks which had recently underperformed the general market. He used leverage, but by now applied concerted discipline to contain his risks. Many of these techniques are used by most successful long/short funds today.[20]

Keynes also employed what would later become a key innovation for individual investors: an "index" representing a group of stocks within an industry. He had used an industrial index in the Provincial portfolio as early as 1932, although Scott objected to the technique.[21]

If Keynes liked a company such as Austin Motors, which appears in several of his portfolios, he added to the position. Unlike in the 1920s, when he was betting on macroeconomic trends in currencies or commodities, his shift in the 1930s was focused on the quality of management at the companies he chose. It also helped that he knew many of the directors and executives of the companies he owned from his many dealings in the City.

This shows his evolution from a "top-down" to a "bottom-up" investment style after 1934:

> As time goes on, I get more and more convinced that the right method in investment is to put large sums into enterprises which one thinks one knows something about and in the management of which one thoroughly believes. It is a mistake to think that one limits one's risk by spreading too much between enterprises about which one knows little and has no reason for special confidence.[22]

If Keynes's loyal attitude toward company management sounds familiar, it is because it was later adopted and echoed by Ben Graham and Warren Buffett. By picking companies with sound

KEYNES'S PETS ⟶ **117**

management and prospects, they concentrated their attention on *individual* stocks instead of market trends, which can be profoundly distracting. Buffett, for example, has remained loyal to companies like Coca-Cola, Dairy Queen, and Geico.

Part of the mantra that value investors like Buffett and Graham embrace is that they buy companies with fairly straightforward business models. They know how these companies make money over time, the likelihood that competitors will erode their market shares, and the reliability of their earnings and dividend streams. Keynes employed this thinking much earlier, holding basic companies like railroads, utilities, shippers, and commodity producers. Throughout the 1930s, despite the fact that the Depression seemed intractable, Keynes kept buying American companies. Between 1934 and 1938, Provincial's net book value of U.S.-based companies rose from $499,878 to $1.3 million, achieving a 7 percent premium above market value by the end of 1938.[23]

Although Provincial's portfolio was extremely volatile for an insurance company, Keynes's wager on an American recovery later paid off. In fact, he never relinquished this idea and increased his position in American preferred and common stock from 32.4 percent in 1929 to nearly 48 percent by 1938.[24] That dedication to what must have looked like a desperate theory went beyond a trench mentality. It was a zeal based on an article of faith.

Keynes Loved Leverage

Keynes's personal portfolio closely mirrored his institutional management. And he frequently ate his own cooking, owning many of the stocks he picked for King's College, Provincial, and National Mutual. His net assets mushroomed along with those of his clients: some 25-fold from 1919 to 1945. The amount of leverage he used also reflected his risk taking during the three phases of his investment career. After initially being burned by his currency speculation in the early 1920s, he reduced his outstanding investment loans to a low of £1,200 in 1925. As he increased his stock holdings from £18,165 in 1929 to £692,059 in 1936, his loans soared from £7,815 to £505,522 during those seven years.[25] Did Keynes know that he was becoming overleveraged during one of the most volatile periods of the century? It's not clear that he knew what direction the 1930s would take, although he appears to have felt comfortable employing such a high-risk strategy in light of his confident outlook for the world economy.

Leverage, of course, magnified his losses during the worst years and nearly cleaned him out in 1920, when he reported a negative net worth of £1,837. He kept on investing, though, doubling his net worth by 1923 (again using 1919 as a base year), and quadrupling it by 1924. When 1929 was over, however, he had lost half of his net worth. Most investors, I imagine, would have called it quits for the next decade or so, or would have stayed in bonds or cash during a largely deflationary decade, which was also a loser's game in terms of real (inflation-adjusted) return. But leverage also amplified his winnings, multiplying his net wealth by a factor of 52 from 1929 to 1945.[26] Table 7.1 shows the relationship between leverage and net assets during his investing career. Note the years in which he was most highly leveraged: 1934–1937. When Keynes saw bargains—during some of the worst years of the 1930s—he borrowed to buy more.

The Measure of Success

By sticking to his investment policy, Keynes not only made money during troubling years (he grew his net worth by a factor of about 25 from 1929 to 1939), but also held onto most of it during World War II. It's also worth noting that Keynes's use of leverage

TABLE 7.1   Keynes's Leverage and Net Worth (£)

Year	Loans	Net Assets
1919	15,498	16,315
1920*	20,837	−1,837
1922	2,720	21,558
1923	1,200	34,364
1924	1,200	63,797
1925	1,200	43,610
1926	2,200	40,800
1927	46,900	44,000
1928	25,790	13,060
1929	14,000	7,815
1930	65,000	12,525
1931	11,965	15,100
1932	19,774	21,722
1933	78,859	55,222
1934	165,343	146,007
1935	188,271	220,619
1936	299,347	506,522
1937	190,035	215,244
1938	106,470	181,547
1939	109,136	199,495
1940	60,655	171,090
1941	28,753	205,281
1942	19,720	254,073
1943	31,643	313,371
1944	46,167	355,310
1945	38,886	411,238

* Through August 1. I've condensed this table to show only his leverage and his total net worth.
Source: Collected Works of JMK, Vol. XII, p. 11.

exploded by nearly a factor of four when he moved heavily into stocks around 1934. From that year through the end of World War II, his financial asset wealth nearly *tripled*.

While Keynes's portfolios fluctuated wildly over the years, the compounding of dividends and appreciation built wealth. Even though he admitted to a few "mistakes" (Elder Dempster was one), he defended nearly all of his picks when challenged. Ironically, his emphasis on "capital profits and accruing income as the measure of success"[27] tended to overshadow the tremendous volatility his portfolios showed. In 1942, with the war at its peak, Keynes wrote

TABLE 7.2 Keynes's Pets (from the Provincial Portfolio)

Keynes bought these companies in the depth of the 1930s because he saw a future for them. Since he was confident that economic conditions would turn around, he saw more people buying cars, going to the theater, and building homes. He was a great fan of Austin Motors in most of his portfolios, and he also favored utilities, shippers, and commodity-related stocks that mined or distributed a wide range of materials.

Stock	Industry
Austin Motors	Autos
British and Dominion Films	Movie production
British Plaster Boards	Building
Carbo Plaster	Building
Elder Dempster	Shipping
Electric Power and Light	Utility
Enfield Rolling Mills	Steel
Grand Union Canal	Transportation
Leyland Motors	Autos
Mortgage Bank of Chile	Banking
South African Torbanite	Mining, resources
Union	South African mining
United Gas Preferred	Utility
Universal Rubber Paviors	Rubber

Scott that "virtually all of our holdings came out right. Now that is what I called a safety-first policy as judged by results."[28]

KEYNESIAN KEYSTONES

An Investment Policy You Can Live With

There are few investors who have the intestinal strength to resist bailing during a market debacle. But that doesn't mean you can't follow Keynes's advice to:

1. Write and stick to a customized investment policy statement. Write down what your goals are. Are you looking for dividend growth and income? Capital appreciation? Companies that can survive during a downturn? Know how much volatility you can stomach, and adjust your portfolio accordingly. Keynes could handle a great deal of volatility, mostly because he remained confident in his stock selection. Will you have the same ability during market declines?

2. Recognize and measure value stocks, and hold them through thick and thin. Some companies will still be able to maintain their business during sour economic conditions. These so-called defensive stocks are typically in healthcare, utilities, and consumer staples. They can be bought at better prices when the market turns south. Identify them, and keep buying them when their prices become more attractive.

3. Don't try to time the market. As I noted in the first chapter in showing how Keynes employed dollar cost averaging, set up a plan to buy shares regularly (perhaps monthly). You can do this through dividend reinvestment plans (DRIPs) with companies that offer them. With these plans, you can buy shares at no commission and reinvest dividend payments in new shares.

4. Balance your portfolio with investments that don't run in the same direction. Remember Keynes's "opposed risks"? You want assets that don't all move in the same direction.

5. Maintain your discipline while others are losing their heads. If you're confident that the companies you own have long-term potential, hold onto them. Keep on buying even when others are selling. You'll get better purchase prices, and your profit margin will be greater when you decide to sell.

These practices are what helped Keynes survive the 1930s, leave behind a fortune, and boost his institutional portfolios. Leverage is always a difficult proposition. Don't go into debt to buy investments unless you can cover the downside and know what you're doing.

If you're a stock investor for the long run, employ the tandem policy of looking for steady dividends and regular appreciation from solid companies. Many mutual funds and exchange-traded funds will do this for you, so you don't need to pick individual stocks. If you choose stocks on your own, make sure you enroll in their dividend reinvestment plans, which allow you to invest your dividends in new shares and not pay a commission on new purchases. And ignore day-to-day fluctuations. Have a long-term goal in mind.

8

Keynes's Heirs

The drain on British reserves was compounded by the lack of an American defense industry. Keynes later claimed that before Lend-Lease Britain spent about $2 billion on capital construction in the U.S. A particularly heavy burden was the $880 billion Britain paid for building aircraft and factories in July 1940. These orders, of course, required payments well in advance of delivery of the goods. British-owned factories were later "sold" to the Americans without payment. Keynes certainly regarded these capital expenditures in the U.S. as moral debts to Britain.

—ROBERT SKIDELSKY[1]

WHEN WORLD WAR II BEGAN TO RAVAGE EUROPE, KEYNES WAS the British Treasury's point man in attempting to open up the wallets of American taxpayers. Although the Lend-Lease program was in full swing, Nazi submarines were sinking ships carrying millions of tons of supplies before they reached England's shores. After visiting Washington to conduct exhausting war finance meetings with a reluctant U.S. government, Keynes was back in London, having regular "treatments" of ice bags on his sore chest, then spending five hours a day at his Treasury office.[2] Although the United States had the largest navy in the world at the time, it didn't have much of an army, a situation that would change after 1941, when Pearl Harbor was bombed. Keynes's life also became more complicated during the blitz, when, while he was having a dinner of duck in the basement kitchen of his London home, a land mine exploded at the opposite end of Gordon Square, smashing doors and windows.[3] He and Lydia retreated to their country home at Tilton while repairs were made. She begged him not to go back to the city, but Keynes felt that he "must do his duty" and worked even harder.[4]

During the intense period when Keynes was focused on financing the war for Britain, he had become something of a celebrity among some of the New Dealers working in the Roosevelt administration. Many of them advocated Keynesian programs to stimulate employment and were able to convince FDR of the necessity of these programs. Keynes had spoken in the United States only a handful of times in the 1930s—once at the University of Chicago on unemployment—but he had gained a following through lecturers at Harvard and other institutions who embraced Keynesian economics. Ever seeking to create a peaceful world order based on stabilized currencies and reduced trade friction, Keynes achieved even greater fame for his role in crafting the Bretton Woods system with Harry Dexter White, which led to the creation of the World Bank and the International Monetary Fund. His work in this area is difficult to imagine, since his heart disease had depleted his energy and he was devoting most of his energy to financing the war effort for Churchill.

The Graham-Buffett Legacy

While how many American economists knew of Keynes's prowess in money management isn't known, these economists took his *General Theory of Employment, Interest and Money*, with its attention to behavioral economics and its search for enterprise value, to heart. Keynes's insights inspired and guided several generations of money managers who applied his principles to portfolio management. During the war, Keynes was still actively managing money for King's College and Provincial. Some of his last missives on the subject capture his long-term "safety first" focus, such as this letter to Provincial's F. C. Scott in 1942:

> There are very few investors, I should say, who eschew the attempt to snatch capital profits at an early date more than I do. I lay myself open to criticism because I am generally trying to look a long way ahead and am prepared to ignore immediate fluctuations. . . . My purpose is to buy securities where I am satisfied as to assets and ultimate earning power and where the market price seems cheap in relation to these.[5]

Keynes's dedication to finding "ultimate earning power" and relative bargains would come to full fruition in the work of Benjamin Graham and his illustrious student Warren Buffett. Like Keynes, Graham, who was teaching at Columbia University, had speculated during the 1920s and hadn't seen the 1929 crash coming. His crafting of new principles—providing formulas for company evaluation—provided much of the quantitative bedrock for the school of value investing.

In his classic popular bible on investing, *The Intelligent Investor*, Graham proclaims that the "investor's primary interest lies in acquiring and holding suitable securities at suitable prices."[6]

Graham makes a clear distinction between the investor and the speculator, whose "primary interest lies in anticipating and profiting from market fluctuations." For Graham, Keynes's "safety first" policy became a "margin of safety," which is "an expected earning power considerably above the going rate for bonds."[7] Building upon this idea, Graham, along with David Dodd, would create a durable edifice for valuing companies, further defining "earning power."

Years later, having learned at the feet of Graham, Warren Buffett touted the book that had ignited Keynes's interest in stocks in the 1920s: Edgar Lawrence Smith's 1924 *Common Stocks as Long-Term Investments*, which Buffett claimed was the "intellectual underpinning of the 1920s stock market mania."[8] Buffett was remarking on Smith's observation that stocks always yielded more than bonds because of retained earnings.

> But, as my mentor, Ben Graham, always used to say, "You can get in way more trouble with a good idea than a bad idea," because you can forget that the good idea has limits. Lord Keynes, in his preface to this book, said, "There is a danger of expecting the results of the future to be predicted from the past."[9]

How much of Keynes's work did Buffett internalize? It's apparent that he took Keynes's many admonitions on short-term speculation and impulsive investing to heart. According to Roger Lowenstein, who incisively tracked Buffett's influences in his *Buffett: The Making of an American Capitalist*, Buffett "read him [Keynes] for his considerable insights into markets."[10]

> For Buffett, Keynes's relevance during the Go-Go era [1960s] was his keen understanding of how crowds could influence

market prices. The stock market *is* a crowd, consisting of whoever is following prices at any given moment.[11]

Buffett took Keynes's idea of "earning power" and expanded upon it. It wasn't enough just to buy a good company at a bargain price. As a buy-and-hold investor, he wanted to know whether the company would have a "long-term durable competitive advantage," something that investment analysts would later prosaically call a "moat" or a layer of protection around the company's ability to consistently hold or grow market share. Unlike Keynes, Graham, and Buffett's partner, Charlie Munger, Buffett would leave the market when he saw prices soaring beyond reasonable levels, which he did in 1969 (Munger stayed in and got burned in the 1973–1974 sell-off).[12] After the market crash, Buffett came back into the market in 1974 to snap up bargains, famously saying, "I felt like a sex-starved man in a harem."[13]

Buffett's record, of course, is legendary, as he has achieved a higher Sharpe ratio (a measure of risk-adjusted performance) "than any stock or mutual fund with a history of more than 30 years," according to researchers Andrea Frazzini, David Kabiller, and Lasse Pedersen from AQR Capital Management.[14] The team explained Buffett's extraordinary returns at his company, Berkshire Hathaway, "by the use of leverage combined with a focus on cheap, safe, quality stocks."[15]

No one would dispute the assertion that Buffett belongs in an elite group of "superinvestors" that also includes Munger and Keynes. Robert Hagstrom, a money manager who has written in depth about Buffett's investing style, says that Buffett and Keynes shared a "focus" method that limited stocks:

to a selected few and [Keynes] relied upon fundamental analysis to estimate the value of his picks relative to price. He liked to keep portfolio turnover at a very low rate. He recognized the importance of diversifying his risks. I believe that, to oppose risk, his strategy was to focus on high-quality predictable businesses with a variety of economic positions.[16]

Buffett's biographer Alice Schroeder told me, "I think you could safely say that Buffett is an admirer of Keynes who has invested time in understanding his body of work."[17]

Having seen Buffett refer to Keynes several times over the past few decades, I wondered how much Keynes actually influenced Buffett and his successful style, so I put the question to him. Although I never connected directly with the investor, his spokesperson Debbie Bosanek bluntly stated, "Keynes had no impact on Mr. Buffett's investing style."[18]

Perhaps Keynes didn't influence Buffett's money management techniques in a direct way, but it's clear that Buffett had some connection to the great economist and his ideas, which resonate in most of Buffett's pronouncements on finding value in companies with solid enterprises.

David Swensen at Yale

David Swensen has been managing Yale University's endowment since 1985 and is known for pioneering the use of alternative investments (Keynes's "opposed risks") to beat other universities' endowment returns for 5-, 10-, and 20-year periods (through 2007).[19] While the fund's overall performance has not been as stellar since the 2008 meltdown, Swensen has been able to contribute more than $1 billion a year to the university's budget, compared to $45 million when he started. Over two decades, Swensen's fund beat the S&P 500 Index by more than five percentage points, a remarkable feat for an active manager.[20]

Swensen cites Keynes frequently in his groundbreaking book *Pioneering Portfolio Management.* (Swensen has also written a much more accessible book for individual investors entitled *Unconventional Success,* in which he also suggests low-cost, passive strategies.) Here's a summary of some of the main points in his portfolio management philosophy and how Keynes influenced his style:

♦ **Market timing can hurt.** "Explicit market timing lies on the opposite end of the spectrum from disciplined portfolio management."[21] In invoking Keynes's observation that market timers often "sell too late and buy too late," Swensen advises that "deliberate short-term deviations from long-term policy targets introduce substantial risks to the investment process."[22] Craft an investment policy statement and stick to it as much as you can. Stick to your guns and don't try to guess where the market is going.

♦ **Real-time rebalancing.** Once you have a plan that identifies set percentages for asset classes, rebalance on a regular basis to maintain those stakes. "Frequent rebalancing activity allows investors to maintain a consistent risk profile and to exploit return-generating opportunities created by excess security price volatility."[23] The market will fluctuate. Try to stick to your plan by selling positions that have appreciated and buying those that have depreciated to maintain your ideal allocation (for example, 60 percent stocks and 40 percent bonds). Rebalancing is the key to maintaining your original allocations in any portfolio. A rising or falling stock market can throw those percentages off—and increase risk—so you need to make yearly adjustments.

♦ **Value investing rests on enterprise value.** Swensen cites Keynes's discussion of "enterprise value" in the *General*

Theory, which would later be quantified by economists James
Tobin and William Brainard in a formula known as Tobin's q,
which expresses the ratio of market value to replacement cost.
"Value investors thrive in environments where 'q' measures
less than one," Swensen wrote.[24] Although you can crunch the
numbers yourself to see whether a company is undervalued
relative to its market price, you're probably better off buying
value-oriented mutual funds that buy these stocks for you.
There is a whole subgenre of investment literature dedicated
to value investing. Just about any book on Warren Buffett or
Graham's *Intelligent Investor* is a good primer.

♦ **Contrarian investing can pay off.** As baseball player Willie
Keeler said of his success at the plate, you need to "keep your
eye clear and hit 'em where they ain't."[25] Keynes essentially
said the same thing, only a bit more elegantly, when fac-
ing down criticism in the late 1930s. Swensen is a tad more
prosaic, since "managers searching among unloved opportunities face greater chances of success, along with almost certain
tirades of criticism."[26] Try to avoid the crowd. You would have
done well to avoid tech stocks in the late 1990s. You could
have made money betting against gold in 2013 or oil in 2008.
The crowd shouldn't be fought, but it's often wrong.

♦ **Don't make any big moves based on shaky assumptions.**
It's incredibly difficult to gauge or predict market movements
in real time. Swensen favors "gradualism" to battle Keynes's
"dark forces of time and ignorance." Swensen further cau-
tions that "Deciding to make radical changes based on highly
uncertain data places too much weight on a shaky foundation."[27] Do your homework before you invest. Don't make
huge shifts into and out of asset classes.

♦ **Be wary of leverage.** Although both Keynes and Swensen
used leverage—and advised against its overuse—Swensen

adds, "Leverage contains the potential to add substantial value and create great harm, posing particular danger to investors pursuing long-term strategies."[28] Don't use leverage unless you know exactly how much money you can lose (and are able to afford to lose) if the market turns against you. It's an extremely sharp double-edged sword.

DANIEL KAHNEMAN, ROBERT SHILLER, AND THE BEHAVIORAL ECONOMICS SCHOOL

As I mentioned in Chapter 6, this group of economists, psychologists, and money managers owes a massive intellectual debt to Keynes and his recognition of the "animal spirits" that move not only markets, but all decision making that's rooted in emotion and impulse. Kahneman, a Nobel Prize winner, makes a masterful study of the subject in his *Thinking, Fast and Slow*. Shiller's ongoing studies of market behavior—his S&P Case-Shiller housing market indexes are worth following—are worth your attention.

While I won't attempt to summarize the bountiful work in this field here, I obtained some advice for investors when I interviewed Dr. Kahneman in early 2012. Given that we consistently make irrational and harmful decisions concerning money, I asked him how can we best avoid the hardwired parts of our brain that lead us astray with money.

♦ "Go with statistics when making [an investment] decision—look for real statistics and not small samples. Ten years [of returns] is better than five."[29] Investors tend to focus on short-term results that not only fail to have predictive value, but are misleading. Past returns are not the same as long-term performance.

- ◆ "Don't make decisions one at a time."[30] All too often, we try to create a portfolio one stock at a time and then become obsessed with those stocks. Take a global view of the entire portfolio and adopt an investment policy. Leave the execution of the policy to someone who understands your needs.

- ◆ "Be more systematic and slow yourself down." Don't try to make decisions by following the news or cable channel bloviators. If you have an idea, sit on it for a few days. If it's rational, it may make sense a week from now—provided you've done your homework.

Jeremy Grantham and the Long View

Like Keynes, Jeremy Grantham employs a keen overview of the supply-demand curve in commodities markets and advises his readers to have at least 30 percent of their holdings in resource-related stocks.[31] Although Grantham is unrelentingly gloomy, most of his warnings are based on population growth and the resulting demand for everything from potable water to grain. In contrast to the behavioral economists, who focus on individual decision making, well-known money manager Jeremy Grantham of Grantham Mayo Van Otterloo frequently cites Keynes when taking on the global picture. Known in the investment community as a "perma bear," Grantham delights and *depresses* his worldwide audience with myriad dour scenarios on resource and food shortages, political instability, and energy production. His quarterly newsletters are broad-ranging white papers on coming food crises, shortages in metals, and the resulting rise in commodity prices.

Grantham's monthly missives on resource depletion and global macro trends echo what Keynes was examining in the years following World War I: would the supply of basic commodities keep up with demand? Grantham is asking the same questions that Keynes explored as an investor, except that he is focusing on issues like growing population, global warming, and, increasingly, demand for food, fertilizer, and fuel.

He's not sanguine about civilization's ability to keep up with the billions of new souls coming into the world, and he echoes the spirit of Keynes, not in theory, but in practice:

> We are badly designed to deal with this problem: regrettably, we are not the efficient species of investment theory, but ill-informed, manipulated, full of inertia, and corruptible. Only once in a blue moon—like World War II—do we perform anywhere near our theoretical capabilities and this time the enemy is amorphous and delivers its attack very, very slowly. But the stakes globally are very high indeed. We must try harder.[32]

Keynes's wartime duties kept him working as a government advisor, yet his global interest was always in peace and economic stability (see the next chapter for his ultimate vision). But Grantham's cri de coeur has even more global impact: if we don't deal with our climate change and resource depletion issues, it won't matter how we invest. Once the material wealth of our planet has been ravaged beyond restoration, stocks and bonds will be worthless pieces of paper.

Jack Bogle's Career Crusade

John C. "Jack" Bogle, like Grantham, has had an abiding interest in Keynes and global investing, although, like the behavioral economists, he has taken a concentrated approach to microeconomics. Not only is Bogle an activist for investor protection, but he's worthy of the Nobel Prize in Economics for pioneering the *index fund*, which Keynes explored in a broad sense in his portfolio management. The concept of the index fund is based on those distracting animal spirits that Keynes warned us about. Rather than timing the market to buy individual stocks and bonds, why not package securities representing entire swaths of the market into funds that hold them passively? The costs are considerably lower than those for buying and selling individual securities, and over time you can achieve market returns minus meager management expenses. Bogle's idea, articulated in his 1951 Princeton University thesis, spawned a more than $2 trillion industry.[33]

You can now find nearly every asset class, from real estate investment trusts (REITs) to commodity funds, in an index mutual fund or exchange-traded fund. In 1974, Bogle founded the Vanguard Group, which rose from obscurity to become one of the largest private money managers on the planet. Vanguard's first index fund was launched in 1975.

The brilliance of an index fund lies in what it doesn't do. It isn't forced to make expensive market-timing decisions. It holds a basket of securities, commodities, or real estate representing a slice (or a large portion) of a particular asset class. That reduces transaction expenses to almost nothing and avoids the frequent mistiming of trades, something that Keynes hoped to avoid when he adopted his long-term investment policy in the 1930s.

Bogle is exuberant in crediting Keynes for his inspiration. When I interviewed him for this book, he said, "Keynes came into my thinking when he said, 'Pay no attention to historical returns; look at the source of the returns.'"[34]

In crediting Keynes and Paul Samuelson, a Keynesian who also won the Nobel Prize in Economics and authored one of the most popular textbooks in history, Bogle says, "I've stood on the shoulders of these two economic giants during so much of my career. . . but of all the reading I did in my field of concentration, it was Keynes's *General Theory*, published in 1936, that has stayed at the forefront of my mind to this very day."[35] (See his foreword for much more detail.)

In reading and digesting Keynes, Bogle said, he realized that there were two types of returns to investors: *speculative* return and *investment* return. The former was what "investors were willing to pay for each dollar of earnings," also measured through the price/earnings ratio; the latter represented Keynes's conception of *enterprise*—the initial dividend yield on stocks plus the subsequent annual rate of earnings growth."[36] Total return is the sum of the two (unless speculative return is a negative number). Under Bogle's formula, for example, if stocks post earnings growth of 5 percent over the coming decade, and the current dividend yield is 2 percent, then the investment return would be 7 percent in nominal terms.[37] (You would have to subtract inflation to calculate *real* returns.) Again, the math is often skewed by the sources of these returns. Speculative fervor isn't sustainable. Dividends and earnings growth are far more durable.

> Over the very long run, it is the *economics* of investing—enterprise—that has been virtually *entirely* responsible for the total return on stocks. The *evanescent* emotions [animal spirits] of investing—speculation—so important over the short run, have ultimately proven to be virtually meaningless.[38]

One of Bogle's greatest gifts to investors, though, is his "cost matters hypothesis," and it's the simplest of all his great contributions to digest. Over time, investment management expenses eat up your returns. You can boost your return by lowering expenses, almost always through passive management and index funds. He found that "the burden of costs has consumed some 65 percent of the returns of the S&P 500 by the year 2000."[39] Costs matter in a big way, so lower them at every juncture in your investing.

KEYNESIAN KEYSTONES

Total Return Is the Objective

As Keynes's heirs have taught us over the past seven decades, every aspect of investing can be a behavioral challenge. We want to time markets to "make a killing" or to latch on to that popular stock that we're sure will be the next Apple or Microsoft. But the most successful investors resist these impulses. They find high-quality enterprises with long-term earnings potential and dividends and hold on to them. They don't buy them at the top of the market. They wait for opportunities and pay attention to book values relative to market prices. None of them are in a hurry to pull the trigger. It makes sense to adopt the strategy of a tortoise and not a hare. Diversification is also important, but be wary of illiquid companies and pay attention to overtrading. In fact, most investors should avoid trading altogether; it will cost too much and impair your returns over time. Employ index funds to capture market returns. Look to long-term trends and hold on to your ideas. Above all, use your investment policy statement as a compass. It may not always point toward true north, but it gives you the direction in which you need to be headed. If you veer off course, you will pay the price.

9

Keynes's Keys to Wealth

Many years ago, Keynes posed a question. For thousands of years, most people had to spend most of their time working just to survive—for food, clothing and shelter. Then, beginning with the Industrial Revolution, unprecedented increases in productivity meant that more and more individuals could be freed from the chains of subsistence living. For increasingly larger portions of the population, only a small fraction of their time was required for the necessities of life. The question was, how would people spend the productivity dividend?

—JOSEPH STIGLITZ[1]

WITH THE WAR OVER, KEYNES HAD GIVEN HIS LAST OUNCE OF vital energy to a conference in Savannah, Georgia, in the spring of 1946 that ironed out the details of the International Monetary Fund and the World Bank, two institutions that thrived after Keynes's passage from the world stage. Although Keynes wasn't entirely happy with the final agreement, and he was exhausted and gravely ill, he prepared a report to the Treasury while he was on his return trip, a six-day ocean voyage. Upon his return to England, he dove into meetings, an article for the *Economic Journal*, and pieces on Isaac Newton and his friend George Bernard Shaw, who was turning 90.[2] He finished some work and headed out to Tilton with Lydia. As usual, he took long walks around the farm, read in the garden, and inspected some of his recent rare book acquisitions.[3] On April 21, the 62-year-old Keynes had another heart attack and died, with Lydia at his side. He was cremated, and his ashes were spread on the downs above Tilton, where he had enjoyed walking with Lydia.[4]

In its obituary of Keynes, the London *Times* stated, "To find an economist of comparable influence, one would have to go back to Adam Smith."[5] Keynes's rival Friedrich Hayek saluted Keynes by writing, "He was the one really great man I ever knew, and for whom I had unbounded admiration. The world will be a very much poorer place without him."[6] England honored Keynes by memorializing him in Westminster Abbey with the prime minister, top Treasury officials, his Bloomsbury friends, his parents, the ballerina Margot Fonteyn, and Lydia in attendance. The only major dignitary missing was Churchill, who was in the United States at the time.[7] Keynes had taken care of Lydia and his family in his will. Upon Lydia's death 35 years later, the bulk of his fortune, which included the papers of Isaac Newton, rare books, and paintings, went to King's College.[8] Although his estate was worth some $22 million (in 2013 dollars) when he died, his legacy to the arts, modern economics, and a more stable global economic climate is incalculable.

Yet Keynes bequeathed much more than a few useful ideas on investing that would stand the test of the Great Depression, several recessions, and two stock market crashes. While his economic legacy is constantly being debated, his contribution to investment management was undeniably revolutionary. He embraced stocks at a time when most institutional portfolio managers were married to bonds and real estate. Even though he was one of the fathers of macroeconomics, he gave up trying to predict where large economies or markets were headed. Instead, he adopted a "small ball" approach that analyzed individual companies. Even more significant is his recognition of "animal spirits" and the role that psychology and mass behavior play in investing and markets. In doing so, he tackled one of the most elusive—and powerful— elements of market-oriented democracies.

The impact that Keynes had as an economist-diplomat is still shaping—and reshaping—the global economy. Yet we can take away some vital lessons on how he invested in a uniquely personal way. Here's where to start.

Keynes's 10 Keys to Wealth[9]

1. **Over time, stocks beat bonds.** Although this is not always true (it depends upon the time period that is being studied), it's *generally* true. From 1926 to 2012, large-company stocks returned an average of 9.8 percent and small-company stocks nearly 12 percent, according to Ibbotson Associates.[10] This compares to 6.1 percent for long-term corporate bonds and 3.5 percent for U.S. Treasury bills.[11] Why do stocks *mostly* beat bonds? Their returns are based on retained earnings and dividends. When times are good, they can boost their dividend payments, and investors will bid up share prices. That doesn't happen with bonds, which provide a fixed income. If you want capital appreciation combined with income, then stocks are still a potent long-term choice for most investors. The bottom line: you won't get wealthy or beat inflation just

owning bonds. You have to take some risk and hold stocks over time.

2. **Speculation is a dangerous game.** Keynes thought he could play the fluctuations in currency and commodity markets with his "superior knowledge." It may be easy enough to digest a ream of statistics and figures about past and present market conditions, but your research may have no predictive value for the future. You may be attracted to the flickering flame of speculation, but keep in mind that speculators rarely have good long-term returns. They may be lucky, but sooner or later their performance is average or below average because they can't possibly know every important fact about market movements. It's a dangerous game.

3. **Probability is not the same thing as certainty.** You may have some excellent analysts' estimates on earnings predictions and bond yields or the latest technical charts on various cycles. That kind of data abounds in an information economy. But, as Keynes discovered, it doesn't protect you from the market's uncertainty about a stock or the economy. This is a gremlin that hurts even the most robust companies—and their stock prices. When there's uncertainty, there are fears and doubts about future economic conditions. Uncertainty that can't be quantified is the sworn enemy of speculators, although savvy investors can turn it into buying opportunities if they've done their homework. Just because a stock like Apple or Exxon Mobil went up last year doesn't mean that it will go up this year. Stock prices represent random points in time, and time moves on. Don't conflate past returns with the likelihood of persistence.

4. **Opposed risks will help balance your portfolio.** You need a mix of assets that are truly uncorrelated during market downturns to give you real diversification. That means

balancing stocks with bonds, real estate, Treasury Inflation-Protected Securities (TIPS), commodities, and other alternatives. Look at the standard deviation of each asset class, which measures its volatility. For stocks, the range is from 20 (large stocks) to 32 (for small companies).[12] The lower the standard deviation, the lower the overall risk of loss. Intermediate-term government bonds have a standard deviation of 5.7; it's 3 for T-bills.[13] Diversification is so important that it's a keystone of investment survival. Bonds may be dreadfully dull, but they were safe harbors in 2008. TIPS may have awful returns as I write this during a low-inflation period, but they will protect you when inflation surges. Not everything will be going up at the same time if you pay attention to opposed risks. Inverse correlation will eventually work for you when markets turn south.

5. **Take advantage of the value quotient.** In the 1930s, when markets were tumbling, Keynes decided to focus on a company's *intrinsic* value. How much would it be worth if it was broken up? What was its franchise/enterprise value, or competitive advantage? What would generate profits in the future? Was it raising its dividends? As Benjamin Graham and Warren Buffett would preach, a well-managed company's value can grow and the market may not always recognize this fact in the market price. Value stocks, which are conveniently packaged in low-cost mutual and exchange-traded funds, should be a staple of your portfolio. Look at a company's book value. Look at its price/earnings ratio. How do these measures compare to those of its peers? What are value investors holding? Look to the future when building a value portfolio. Can you hold a stock for 10 years?

6. **Dividends don't lie.** They are paid every quarter, and they represent a share of a company's earnings. When Keynes

loaded up on utility companies in the 1930s, he did so to buffer his portfolio and grab an income stream. Find companies that are raising their dividends on a regular basis; these are among the healthiest companies on the planet. They are durable and steady. As with the value stocks, you can find them pooled in dividend growth funds. Will a company keep paying you dividends through thick and thin? How much is it increasing its dividend from year to year, or is it cutting its payment? What's the likelihood that dividend payments will rise? Keep in mind that the highest dividend yields are from companies that the market considers the riskiest investments. Be a tortoise: slow and steady wins the race.

7. **Don't move with the crowd.** Being a contrarian pays off. Find healthy, unloved companies at bargain prices and stick with them. Don't try to time the market, but look for opportunities to buy companies with a good "moat," that is, protection from the competition. You'll do much better by finding underdogs and holding them than by buying today's popular stocks and hoping that they'll gain value. Keynes found the latter method to be a loser. It's still true. Don't be sucked into the beauty contest. There are hundreds of stocks that don't win the day, but they're still winners over time. The market is efficient in pricing securities most of the time, but not all the time. Why not take advantage of the market's mistakes? Pick stocks or sectors when they are out of favor. Look up the key sectors in the S&P 500 Index at the end of a year and pick the laggards, or the "dog" Dow Industrial stocks that did poorly the previous year. If you can go against the grain, you can boost your long-term total return.

8. **Invest for the long term.** Even if the current environment looks dismal, if you have a long-range investment policy— and if it still works for you given your appetite for risk—by

all means stick with it. Rebalance once a year to ensure that you're on course and aren't loading up in any one asset class. Take some money off the table by selling some of your winners and buying more of undervalued assets. If you plan to use leverage, use it sparingly. You can get into trouble awfully fast (hello, margin calls!) because the market moves at the speed of light. The greatest danger to any investor is acting impulsively. The market can throw off any number of false signals and panics in a heartbeat. With high-frequency trading, the volatility is even worse for modern investors. Keep to your investment policy.

9. **Invest passively.** Given that you can't divine the state of long- or short-term expectations because animal spirits are doing their mischief, put most of your money in cheap index funds. You need only a handful of them to produce a diversified portfolio. Why is an index fund your best friend? An index *is* the market. Most investors guess badly when it comes to market swings, so why not get what most of the market is getting? Even when active managers have a good year, it may be the result of luck and they can't repeat it. Even Keynes got burned in the late 1920s and late 1930s. Between 2009 and 2012, the S&P 500 Index outperformed 64 percent of actively managed funds (through 2012), 75 percent of mid-cap funds were beaten by the S&P MidCap 400 Index, and 63 percent of small-cap funds were bested by the S&P SmallCap 600 Index.[14] The cost difference that index funds offer is always in your favor and allows you to build more wealth. Actively managed funds charge you an average of 1.3 percent of your assets under management annually.[15] That's in addition to transactions expenses to buy and sell securities, timing errors, and sales charges. Index fund expenses run as low as *0.06* percent annually. The savings go right into your pocket.

10. **Drink more champagne!** This is said to have been Keynes's
one regret (and last words)—that he had not enjoyed life
more and drunk more bubbly. The object of investing is
to ensure *prosperity*, not to become obsessed with making
money. Prosperity isn't necessarily having a four-car garage
filled with toys or a closet stuffed with clothes and shoes. It's
the hope for a secure and comfortable future. Everybody has
a different idea of what that is, but it shouldn't be a debilitat-
ing obsession. When Keynes first started earning money, he
either gave it away, bought books or paintings, took vacations, funded arts activities, or donated it to his college. Here
was a genius who truly loved life, people, and the world.
His world, which was constantly in turmoil, bombed and
blistered by monumental wars and despair, didn't sink him.
Keynes kept on trying to improve the world he knew with
his mind and spirit. That's his spiritual legacy, not the money
he made investing or the economic theories he devised. So
put your investing on autopilot with a sound plan that meets
your goals and monitor it once a year. Then go out and live.

KEYNES'S LAST PORTFOLIO

The following stocks were held in Keynes's personal portfolio
when he died in 1946. You'll see a lot of familiar names. As I've
mentioned earlier, if he liked a stock, he bought it for nearly
every one of his portfolios. This was Keynes's most forward-
looking allocation. We see his optimism for the future after
World War II. As he was drafting the template for the new economic world order through the Bretton Woods Accords, he was
also bullish on gold, shipping, metals, railroads, manufacturing,
airplanes, and consumer goods. Even though Europe and Japan
were devastated, he saw a brighter future for world trade.

U.S. Stocks

American Cities Power, American General, Associated
Dry Goods, Central States Electric, Chicago Corp., Climax
Molybdenum, Tri-Continental, United Corp.

Non-U.S. Stocks

London & Northeast Railway, London Midland & Scottish Rail,
Bristol Aeroplane, Hawker Siddeley Aircraft, Lancashire Cotton,
Lever Brothers/Unilever, Leyland, Lancashire Steel, Richard
Thomas & Baldwins, Gold Exploration/Finance of Australia,
Selection Trust, Union, Elder Dempster Lines, Peninsular &
Oriental Steam Navigation, Royal Mail Lines, Union Castle Mail
Steamship

Source: Probate account from Buckmaster & Moore (Keynes's broker), May 6,
1946, King's College Archives.

Keynes's Winning Combination: Gumption and Flexibility

It's hard to stick to your plan when the waves are lapping over
your deck. And it's equally difficult to abandon a strategy that
doesn't seem to be working. By shifting into stocks in the 1920s
and getting out of currencies and commodities, Keynes was able
to build wealth, but it certainly required a lot of gumption.

Keynes held on to his carefully selected stocks—representing
pieces of nearly every major part of the economy—throughout the
1930s and into World War II. Had he sold those stocks at certain
crisis points (after the crash of 1929 or the downturn of 1937), his
returns would have been awful. Here's what he gained by holding
on: he caught the upswing of some great rebounds. Here are two
little-known rallies that occurred during what seemed to be the

worst possible times that accounted for the lion's share of Keynes's total gains:

1932–1937. Few people realize that this was the second-greatest rally of the twentieth century, after the 1921–1929 boom. U.S. stocks alone rose nearly 280 percent during the 1930s rebound. Keynes stayed in the market throughout the decade, although he took some punishing losses from 1937 up until World War II.

1942–1946. This was another incredibly counterintuitive call. The Germans were bombing the heck out of London, British ships were being sunk by the hundreds, and things looked pretty grim for Europe until D-Day in 1944. Keynes, however, managed to hold on to his portfolio. U.S. stocks rose 122 percent during that time, so he finished strong in his stewardship of his own—and institutional—funds, according to the Leuthold Group.[16]

The theme here is to pick high-quality stocks or hold a diversified portfolio and look down the road. Will these stocks be worth owning in better times? How will a rebounding economy affect their earnings? Keynes saw the future (as you can see in his last portfolio) as being in aircraft, steelmaking, shipping, energy, and metals. He bought these companies at great prices when war was raging in two hemispheres. Not only did he have the ability to look ahead, but he put his money where his optimism was.

The Legacy of a Better Life

When Keynes put the finishing touches on the Bretton Woods agreement, which was designed to prevent trade and currency wars (the fixed currency component was abandoned in the 1970s), his goal was that "social progress and economic prosperity should be the overriding mission of the post-war era," according to Andre Malabre Jr. in *Lost Prophets*.[17] Today, we're still trying to achieve the same goals despite a punishing recession and a middle class that is losing ground across the world because of inequality in income. We're all struggling to craft our own Bretton Woods for the future.

As the basis of all his ideas on economics and investing, what Keynes wanted for the world was "a decent level of consumption for everyone; and . . . the occupation of our energies in the non-economic interests of our lives."[18] It must have seemed like a utopian goal when he wrote this in 1937, yet "the maintenance of prosperity" was at the top of his social agenda. He wasn't much interested in the redistribution of wealth the way his Fabian socialist friends like George Bernard Shaw were. Nor was he ready to jettison capitalism in the face of social unrest. Furthermore, he was just as repulsed by fascism and totalitarian communism as Hayek was.

Keynes advised us that, even in the throes of economic chaos, we need to refocus on the long view, to try to achieve a life in which we are working less and spending more time in leisure pursuits. Even though he was one of the most in-demand workaholics of his time, Keynes still managed to find time for the theater, the ballet, his farm, and socializing with one of the most interesting social circles of that time. As a virtual upstart in contrast to the established orthodox school of classical economics, Keynes derided the notion that economics was a religion, although he thought the science had an ethical foundation. In his 1924 speech "The End of Laissez-Faire," Keynes debunked the notion that "individuals have a prescriptive 'natural liberty' in their economic activities. There is no 'compact' conferring perpetual rights on those who Have or on those who Acquire."[19] Keynes would have been critical of CEOs who enrich themselves at the expense of shareholders or hedge fund managers who get unneeded tax breaks and plunder markets. He pointed to "great inequalities of wealth" that came about because particular individuals could "take advantage of uncertainty and ignorance."[20]

Even when Keynes was speculating in currencies and commodities, he *still* lobbied for "deliberate control of the currency and of credit by a central institution."[21] For Keynes, regulation and oversight, not the anything-goes world of economic libertines, was a road toward shared prosperity. Prior to the New Deal era, there was little regulation of financial markets and public companies. When I looked at annual reports from the 1920s during research for my book *Merchant of Power*, these documents were only a handful of pages long and told you very little about the companies. There was almost no transparency and accountability.

When nobody is looking, those with power, advantage, and capital will run amok, often leading to crashes when the avaricious excesses can't be contained. These eras of scant financial policing are often preceded by huge inequalities in wealth, which Keynes referred to indirectly in 1924 and more pertinently in the 1930s. John Kenneth Galbraith, in appraising the reasons for the crash of 1929, had at the top of his list "the bad distribution of income," citing the fact that the richest 5 percent of Americans had twice the income of the rest of the population in the years following World War II.[22] The most affluent can spend only so much and can't buoy an economy. When financial calamity comes, everybody cuts back, and it's universally painful. This is the human face of Keynesian economics that constantly imperils prosperity.

With the world reeling from one war to the next with the Great Depression in between, it would have been easy for Keynes to trash the capitalist system. The "invisible hand" couldn't seem to defeat the forces of ignorance and despair during the 1930s. It was only when World War II came along, ironically, that the largest economies roared back to life, forever changing the balance of power in the world.

Nevertheless, Keynes never stopped pondering the "economic problem" as one of the great questions of humanity. How could we ensure prosperity, keeping in mind the uncertainty and calamity of market economics? Was more government control the answer? Was it technology? Was it population control? As a student of Malthusian economics, Keynes always believed that controlling population would make a difference. He also saw technology and productivity gains eventually becoming triumphant in giving us more time for ourselves and less for the workplace.

Just as the global economy became unhinged and opened the door for the most disastrous war in history, Keynes predicted that we would become "eight times better off in an economic sense in 100 years."[23] In his hopeful 1930 essay "Economic Possibilities for Our Grandchildren," he tackles the economic problem with elegance:

> The strenuous purposeful money-makers may carry all of us along with them into the lap of economic abundance. But it will be those peoples, who can keep alive, and cultivate into a fuller perfection, *the art of life itself* [italics mine] and do not sell themselves for the means of life, who will be able to enjoy abundance when it comes.[24]

In terms of economic growth, Keynes's math, extrapolated to 2013, came pretty close. But his calculation of drastically reduced weekly work hours did not.[25] Robert and Edward Skidelsky, in tracking Keynes's forecast, noted that we're not working the 20 hours a week that the economist had predicted for the present. If anything, middle-class workers are putting in more hours—with two spouses or partners in the workplace—than they did 30 years ago. Inflation is one reason. The cost of homes, college educations, and medical expenses are another. There is more aggregate wealth from Boston to Beijing than at any other point in history, but it's unequally distributed. Middle-class households are losing ground as a result of wages having stagnated more than a decade ago. In fact, a whole subgenre of economic writing and research has extensively detailed this fallback in recent years.

The Skidelskys imply that poor use of human capital is at fault: "The greatest waste now confronting us is not one of money, but of human possibilities." We need to put our human resources, talents, experience, and wisdom to better use in securing a more prosperous life that emphasizes well-being over material acquisition and pure wealth. Keynes said it even better in 1933: "Once we allow ourselves to be disobedient to the test of an accountant's profit, we have begun to change our civilization."[26]

Saving and investing can yield a more prosperous future, but they need to be directed toward a mutually beneficial purpose. Profit and growth are important, yet these are not the things that sustain life, but merely the tools to finance it. Although every portfolio should be based on an ethical plan that works for us and our loved ones, it can't survive in a vacuum. It should reflect our values and ideals. It can add to prosperity, but it won't ensure it. For that, we have to look deep into our animal spirits to divine what really matters.

Epilogue

The Once and Future Keynes

We do not need the new Keynes; we need
the old Keynes, suitably updated. He will not
be our sole guide to the economic future,
but he remains an indispensable guide.

—ROBERT SKIDELSKY[1]

WHEN I APPROACHED PAUL KRUGMAN IN LATE JANUARY 2013 AT a lecture in Chicago, I asked him if he had known about Keynes's prowess in investing. "No," he replied, "but have you seen my introduction to [a recent edition of] his *General Theory [of Employment, Interest and Money]*?"[2] I had, and, somewhat disappointed, moved on as a horde of well-wishers waited in line for him to sign his books. What Krugman did know about Keynesian theory was that it *wasn't* being employed to save Europe from economic turmoil or to create jobs in the United States. Even as President Obama was calling for more Keynesian stimulus in the guise of infrastructure and education spending, half of the country was still at odds with him. Not only was Keynes very much alive, but his ideas lived on to tease, teach, and torment us.

Krugman was lambasting the current state of affairs by pointing to the antithesis of Keynesian theory, *austerity* economics, which was ravaging most of the eurozone, forcing draconian spending cutbacks and massive unemployment. What Krugman called the "Keynesian compact" of ramping up investment and spending during slumps was mostly dead on arrival after the Obama stimulus plan of 2009 had run its course (which I detailed in my previous book, *The Audacity of Help*). "As Keynes said three quarters of a century ago, 'the boom, not the slump, is the right time for austerity'"[3] Krugman said during his Chicago speech.

Austerity may *sound* like a rational cure for ailing, overindebted economies emerging from debt bubbles, but it has proved to be like administering mercury as an antibiotic. It may well dispatch the disease, but at the expense of poisoning the patient. Moreover, austerity isn't effective for reviving economic growth. Krugman noted that a study done by the International Monetary Fund— one of Keynes's brainchildren—showed that in 173 cases of fiscal austerity programs from 1978 to 2009, the programs led to *contracted* economic growth and higher unemployment.[4]

The growing ranks of the jobless and the declining middle class also lead to greater inequality. With this skewed flow of wealth, if there is economic growth, it flows disproportionately to the upper 5 percent of the population. Because the superrich can make use of corporations, offshore tax havens, and lower tax rates on dividends and capital gains, they get to keep more of their income, notes Joseph Stiglitz in *The Price of Inequality*. All of this is exacerbated by the fact that "for a third of a century American workers have seen their standard of living first stagnate, then erode."[5]

From a Keynesian perspective, inequality, austerity, and erosion of living standards are a negative scenario for investors. They put a foot on the throat of economic growth, upward mobility, and ultimately the stock prices of companies that gain their long-term profits from a shrinking consumer economy. Without aggregate demand, cash registers don't ring and earnings don't accelerate. When governments spend money to bolster private-sector employment—as Skidelsky notes happened during the Bretton Woods years prior to the mid-1970s—economic growth (in the world) ranged from 4 percent to 7 percent, for an average rate of 4.8 percent. In the anti-Keynesian "Washington consensus" period after 1980, growth declined to 3.2 percent.[6] It may eventually be half that in 2013. Does this mean that there was a visible Keynesian cycle at play during the Bretton Woods years? Skidelsky thinks so, and observes that it was supported by massive spending for the space race, infrastructure building, education, and even Cold War armaments. High inflation and the Vietnam War put an end to that boom, but that doesn't mean that Keynesian stimuli on a large scale wouldn't work again. The austerity debate, however, has become so bitter that even the word *Keynes* has become political poison for a large segment of the American political class. Yet there's no denying that the raft of austerity measures imposed on Southern Europe since 2008 had made stocks from those countries terrible investments, in addition to compounding people's misery through lack of demand and rising unemployment (the eurozone economy was improving as this goes to press). And the idea that raising the sovereign debt load during a downturn hurts a country's chances for recovery may be a fallacy.

Ironically, China, the world's second largest economy, is growing at a near-double-digit pace and employs Keynesianism on a large scale in its attempt to accommodate the largest rural-to-urban migration in human history. The country is building subways, airports, high-speed rail, and entire cities at a breakneck pace. In the process, it's employing hundreds of millions of people and raising their standards of living. Although China is still a repressive and highly unequal society, it's making progress, but not by imposing austerity.

What Needs to Be Done: Future Investment Needed

If you were an investor, would you invest in a country or a company that stifles growth, creativity, education, and infrastructure building? Or would you place your dollars in an environment that places a high premium on public facilities, high-quality education, and increases in human capital? Investment is the linchpin for spending, but incentives are needed. The following are a few points as you consider the global investment climate:

+ **What countries give their upper class incentives to invest in socially productive enterprises and businesses?** As author and labor lawyer Thomas Geoghegan writes, "We have to get the *rich* to invest . . . not save, not speculate in financial instruments, but invest in widgets we can wrap and ship and sell abroad."[7]
+ **How does a country generate investment and sustainable growth?** "Keynes was right to argue that the state has a critical role to play in facilitating investment," notes Vince Cable, British secretary of state for business, innovation and skills.[8] How much money is spent on medical research, technology, education, and overall innovation? Where are the new patents coming from? What companies foster the imagination and create products and services that enhance the quality of life? There's a reason why companies like Apple and Google have maintained such high stock prices and market valuations. How can an economic climate sustain companies like these in the future?

- **How does a country discourage debt and encourage investment?** Robert Kuttner claims that one of the reasons for the 2008 collapse was the "privatized Keynesian non-public debt."[9] From Wall Street to Main Street, massive debt financed unsustainable lifestyles and speculation. In his *General Theory*, Keynes proposed limiting the liquidity of investments to reduce short-term speculation. The United Kingdom is eyeing a "Robin Hood tax" on banking profits. A small tax on trading transactions is another possible route.

- **How can countries (and companies) create a better model of sustainable social capitalism?** More than ever, we need to pay attention to diminishing resources and global warming. The impacts are devastating. Speculation in commodities markets drives up food prices and creates despair and unrest in the developing world. While Americans were dealing with the implosion of the real estate and credit markets in 2007–2008, 115 million more hungry people fell prey to a 42 percent gain in food prices.[10] Commodities markets clearly need limits on rampant trading. Resource overconsumption can no longer be ignored. The planet is not a limitless breadbasket.

If economics is the science of resource scarcity, then it seems reasonable that a new form of it is needed that straddles the anti-debt/antigovernment Hayekian model and the government stimulus of Keynes. A third way is sustainable "spiritual" capitalism that looks beyond what Al Gore calls the "short-termism" of speculation and quick profits. "Do we want to allocate resources to short-termism?" Gore asks.[11] In other words, how can we better focus our economic power to create long-term well-being for the majority of the population?

Markets can be used to create incentives the same way taxes can impose disincentives on carbon dioxide, vices, and unbridled speculation. Ultimately, markets can be employed to ensure our future on this planet. "A society has one higher task than to consider its goals," wrote John Kenneth Galbraith in *The Affluent Society*, and that is "to reflect on its pursuit of happiness and harmony and its success in expelling pain, tension, sorrow and the ubiquitous case of ignorance. It must, so far as this may be possible, ensure its own survival."[12]

As investors and global citizens, we can do much better than just survive. We can embrace the shared prosperity that Keynes hoped would come from solving the economic problem. All it takes is our concerted, communal investment—of our capital, time, and spirit.

A

Visiting Keynes Country and His Other Sources of Wealth

In Cambridge, the ancient university town where Keynes was born and grew up, you don't have to go far to see the economist's thumbprint. There's a Keynes House sitting astride the funky, neo-Victorian Judge Business School. His parents' home was on Harvey Road, just south of the campus. His name is on the Arts Theatre, which he founded and financed. Then there's the university's Fitzwilliam Museum, which received most of the paintings and manuscripts that he bought and collected over the years.

As you have no doubt gleaned from Keynes's extensive financial activity, he was a shrewd investor. He bought high-quality stocks at bargain prices and held on to them during the worst markets of the century. He also employed this same strategy when buying art and rare manuscripts, although he initially bought these items for the pure joy of seeing and owning them (aesthetics for its own sake was a strong piece of his ethical training from G. E. Moore). Although it's nearly impossible to value what he bought, since most of his artwork was never put on the auction block, it's highly conceivable that this part of his portfolio was worth far more than his financial assets, perhaps in the tens of millions if the pieces had made it to an auction house for sale. I'm hardly an art appraiser, so this is a wild guess on my part.

Keynes started buying major artists near the end of World War I, as soon as he obtained some disposable income. He was always generous to his Bloomsbury friends, buying paintings from Vanessa Bell and Duncan Grant. One of the Bloomsbury works—a delightful painting (probably by Grant) of Keynes peeking from behind a curtain to offer Lydia flowers after a ballet performance—graces the reading room of the King's College Archives. When I was doing my research, I was moved by the extent to which archivist Patricia McGuire had turned the room into a minishrine to the Bloomsbury group. Not only did she have Keynes's papers, but she had shelved books from E. M. Forster and manuscripts from T. S. Eliot, among others. I saw (they were in a case behind my work table) some of the original drawings from Eliot's *Old Possum's Book of Practical Cats,* the whimsical set of poems that were turned into a smash musical by Andrew Lloyd Webber.

Cambridge itself is a potpourri: a medieval college town bustling with students and dons on bicycles (the two-wheeled traffic seemed to be greater than the four-wheeled kind) and a working community full of restaurants, a market, chapels with nightly choir concerts, and modern researchers busy at work on everything from the origin of the universe (Stephen Hawking) to drug development. Yet when you leave the din of the town and enter the courtyards of the ancient colleges, modernity disappears into the quiet solitude of colleges whose traditions haven't changed much in centuries. Students still wear robes (at certain times).

The bells of the chapels still ring. It was so quiet in the King's College Archives, which had a splendid view of the magnificent chapel built by Henry VI, that I could hear a faucet dripping in a water closet—a *floor below*. This was part of Keynes's world, a pensive retreat from the frenetic London streets, although his home on Gordon Square in Bloomsbury is fairly sedate compared to the rest of London. I was moved to tears hearing the beautiful, world-class King's College Chapel Choir perform in that sacred space, a group that I've listened to from afar every Christmas on the radio.

Keynes had a great eye for art and manuscripts and bought some great pieces for what today would be considered a pittance. Here's just a sampling of what he owned:

- Several pieces by Cubists George Braque and Pablo Picasso (Picasso was in his outer circle of friends)
- Impressionist works that included a study for *A Sunday Afternoon on the Island of La Grande Jatte* by Georges Seurat; drawings by Degas and Ingres; four paintings by Cezanne; and one Matisse
- Contemporary paintings (for that time) by William Roberts, Walter Sickert, and Matthew Smith
- The original manuscript of *Principia Mathematica* and other papers of Isaac Newton
- Rare classic books by Aristotle, St. Augustine, Bacon, Copernicus, Dryden, Galileo, Hobbes, Erasmus, Kepler, Milton, More, and Virgil
- First editions of Milton's *Paradise Lost*, Spenser's *The Faerie Queen*, and Ben Jonson's *Plays*.

Keynes's legacy went far beyond what he left to the university and the arts community of his time. The theater that he founded in the middle of Cambridge still produces plays (a thriller was playing when I was in town). Just as Keynes's contributions to global economic stability and investing continue to inform us, his cultural legacy continues. He was truly a man for all seasons.

The Independent Investment Company Portfolio

KEYNES AND OSWALD FALK MANAGED THE INDEPENDENT Investment Company (IIC) portfolio jointly from 1924 until a conflict in management philosophy created a rift between the two friends in the early 1930s. At first, the firm was successful, raising its capital to £500,000 in 1926 from an initial £350,000 in 1924.

By March 1929, appreciation was £63 for every £100 share.[1] Then Keynes and Falk moved in opposite directions on what strategy to embrace. In the summer of 1929, Falk had taken the view that U.S. stocks represented the future of investing and had invested accordingly for himself and clients, often failing to inform Keynes. According to Moggridge, Keynes held firmly to the idea that "a major slump was in the offing" after the market crashed that fall.[2] The two never quite resolved their differences and drifted apart as the 1930s ground on, although Keynes gradually became more of an investor in U.S. shares during that dark decade.

Nevertheless, this portfolio profile from June 30, 1925, represents Keynes and Falk working in unison. It was the Roaring Twenties, and a stock frenzy was gripping the United States. Catalog retailer Sears, Roebuck opened its first retail store at the height of a new, consumer-focused era of merchandising and retailing. The Chrysler Corporation was founded. The pro-business president Calvin "Silent Cal" Coolidge was inaugurated. F. Scott Fitzgerald had just published his classic novel *The Great Gatsby* about the sudden riches and embedded conflicts of the era, while Adolf Hitler had published *Mein Kampf.* [3]

Keynes was already one of the most famous economists in the world, but he was still a decade away from writing his masterpiece, *The General Theory of Employment, Interest and Money*. Yet this portfolio displayed his unwavering confidence in commodities, minerals, shipping, engineering, and transportation. If this portfolio had a theme, it would be "building and growth in the modern age." Commodities were again moving around the world to build cities, factories, stores, and growing suburbs. Scarcely half a decade after the end of World War I, international trade among the Americas, Asia, and Western Europe was booming. The London Underground was expanding (one of IIC's largest holdings was Underground Electric bonds).

There were few commodities that escaped Keynes and Falk's attention. Everything from Portland cement to zinc is in this portfolio. Keynes's extensive knowledge of the commodities markets informed his purchases of companies that derived profits from coffee, coal, copper, oil, nickel, and tin. A handful of "technology" companies such as General Electric and Eastman Kodak were also represented. This was an active portfolio that played on major growth trends as the world increasingly built up its cities, transportation networks, and infrastructure.

Other than focusing on the growth theme of the mid-1920s, the portfolio displays Keynes's preference for "leader" companies with durable franchises, solid cash flow, and steady dividends. Of course, while this approach didn't work in the early 1930s, it's a decent strategy when national economies are on the upswing. As someone who took a long view on economic trends, Keynes fervently believed that there would be a turnaround after the devastation of the 1930s—and later World War II. By the time he died in 1946, IIC "funds underlying the ordinary shares had almost returned to their original issue price," writes Moggridge.[4] Keynes's faith in his original model had paid off. He had largely shrugged off the pessimism of animal spirits during one of the worst decades for investors and prevailed.

The Independent Investment Company Limited Valuation of Investments on 30th June 1925

		Value at or Under Cost	Middle Prices 30/6/25	Present Value
£ 9,900	Brazillian Government 7.5% Coffee Security Loan	£11,103	£110.10 0.	£10,959.
£ 3,050	London Midland & Scottish Rly. 4.5% Pref. 1925.	3,049	- - -	3,050.
£ 1,000	London Midland & Scottish Rly. 5% Pref. 1926.	999	99. 0. 0.	990.
£ 3,000	Metropolitan Rly. Consolidated Stock	2,132	70.10. 0	2,115.
£ 500	Southern Rly. 5% Pref. 1926	501	99. 0. 0.	495.
£ 5,000	Associated Portland Cement Mfrs. Ordinary	4,708	14. 3.	3,563.
£ 4,000	Borax Consolidadted Co. Defd. Ordinary	8,551	1.17. 6.	7,600.
£ 1,500	British Insulated & Helsby Cables Ordinary	3,877	3. 2. 6.	4,688.

(continued on next page)

The Independent Investment Company Limited Valuation of Investments on 30th June 1925 *(continued)*

		Value at or Under Cost	Middle Prices 30/6/25	Present Value
£ 4,000	British Ropes Ltd Ordinary	5,831	1.17. 9	5,662.
£ 3,000	Brunner Mond & Co. Ltd. Ordinary	5,831	1.17. 9.	5,662.
£ 1,000	Callenders Cable Construction Co. Ltd. Ord.	338	6. 7.5.	331.
£ 2,000	Cellulose Holdings & Investment Co 7% Partc. and 1st Mtgs. Deb.	2,335	115. 0. 0.	2,300.
£ 3,000	Courtaulds Ltd. Ordinary	5,305	5. 5. 0.	15,750.
£ 2,000	Debenhams Ltd. 10% Cum. Prefd. Ordinary Shares	2,566	1. 7. 0.	2,700.
4,000	Dunlop Rubber Co. 10% C. Pref. Shares	4,509	1. 2. 6.	4,500.
£ 6,000	Dunlop Rubber Co. 8% 1st. Mtge. Deb.	6,508	104.xd.	6,240.
£ 2,000	James Finlay & Co. Ltd. Ordinary	4,943	3.11. 3.xd	7,125.
£ 5,000	General Electric Co. Ltd. Ordinary	5,224	1. 5. 0.	6,250.
£ 1,500	Imperial Tobacco Co. (of G.B & Ireland) Ordinary	5,527	5. 1. 6.	7,613.
£ 5,000	Jute Industries 9% Cum Pref.	4,953	18. 0.	4,500
250	Liebigs Extract of Meat Co. Ordinary bearer	3,197	15. 7. 6.	3,844.
200	Manbre Sugar & Malt Co. Deferred	2,018	11.10. 0.	2,300.
£ 2,500	Mather & Platt Ltd. Ordinary	6,912	2. 6. 3.	5,781.
£ 2,500	Mond Nickel Co. Ltd. Ordinary	4,743	2. 0. 0.	5,000.
£ 8,000	Nobel Industries Ordinary	9,403	1. 3. 6.xd	9,400.
1,100	Swedish Match Co. Ordinary New "B" shares of 100 kroner each	8,595	10. 8. 9.	11,481.
£10,000	Underground Electric 6% Income Bonds	10,216	98. 0. 0.	9,800.
£ 600	Wall Paper Manufacturers Ordinary	712	1. 6.10.5.xd	806
£ 4,000	Wall Paper Manufacturers Deferred	2,675	1. 7. 0.	5,400.
£ 1,350	Whiteaway Laidlaw & Co. Ltd. Ordinary	2,789	.1.12. 6.	2,194.

The Independent Investment Company Limited Valuation of Investments on 30th June 1925 *(continued)*

		Value at or Under Cost	Middle Prices 30/6/25	Present Value
£3,800	Australian Estates & Mortgage Co. Ordinary	5,186	.1 .1 3.xd	4,781.
£ 4,500	Forestal Land Timber & Railways Co. Ordinary	5,186	1. 1. 3.xd	4,781.
3,000	Lake View Investment Trust Ltd.	3,009	18. 9.	2,813
£ 1,000	New Zealand & Australian Land Co. Ordinary	1,675	200. 0. 0.	2,000.
£ 5,000	Amalgamated Anthracite Collieries Ltd.	5,727	17. 0.	4,250.
£ 5,000	Sir W.G. Armstrong Whitworth Co. 5.5% 3 year notes.	4,938	99. 7. 6.	4,969.
£ 2,000	Babcock & Wilcox Ltd. Ordinary	4,840	2. 8. 9.	4,837.
£ 600	Bolckow Vaughan & Co. Ltd. 8% 1st. Deb. 1925.	608	85. 0. 0.	510.
£ 4,400	Bolckow Vaughan & Co. Ltd. 8% 1st. Deb. 1930.	4,556	95. 0. 0.	4,180.
£ 3,000	Denaby & Cadeby Main Collieries Ltd. Ordinary	2,858	15. 7.5.	2,344.
£ 2,000	Dorman Long & Co. Ltd. 8% Hon. Cum. Pref. Ord	2,141	16. 3	1,625.
£ 2,500	Horden Collieries Ltd. Ordinary	5,629	1. 6.10.5.	3,359.
£ 3,000	Pease & Partners Ltd. Ordinary	3,715	13.1.5	1,969.
£ 4,000	Platt Bros. & Co. Ltd. Ordinary	6,848	1. 5. 7.5.	5,125.
£ 1,500	Stewarts & Lloyds Ltd. Deferred	3,252	1.14. 4.5.	2,578.
25,000	Burma Corp. Ordinary Shares of Rs. 10 each	14,514	14. 9.	18,438.
£ 2,000	Gopeng Consolidated Ltd. Ordinary	4,377	2. 6.10.	4,683.
£ 2,000	Kamunting Tin Dredging Ltd. Ordinary	5,485	2.17. 2.	5,717.
£ 5,000	National Smelting Co. 7% 1st Mtge. Deb.	5,297	98.10. 0.xd	4,925.
10,000	Pahang Consolidated Co. Ltd. Shares	5,569	10. 9.	5,375.

(continued on next page)

The Independent Investment Company Limited Valuation of Investments on 30th June 1925 *(continued)*

		Value at or Under Cost	Middle Prices 30/6/25	Present Value
£ 2,000	Southern Perak Dredging Co. Ltd.	4,659	2. 9.8.	4,967
£ 2,000	Tekka Ltd Shares	1,794	18. 1.	1,808.
£ 2,000	Tekka Taiping Ltd. Ordinary	2,411	1. 2. 3.	2,225.
£ 3,000	Zinc Corporation 20% Cum. Pref.	8,042	3. 1. 3.75.	9,197.
£10,000	Anglo Persian oil Co. Ltd. 6.5% 5 year notes.	10,103	102. 5. 0	10,225.
£ 1,000	Burmah Oil Co. Ltd.	5,466	4.18. 9.xd	4,937.
£ 5,000	Shell Transport & Trading Co. Ltd. Ord. Bearer	21,815	4. 7. 6.	21,875.
£ 5,000	Eagle Oil Transport Co. Ltd. 12 year 7% notes (Reg.)	5,095	100. 0. 0.xd	5,000.
£ 3,000	Eagle Oil Transport Co. Ltd. 12 year 7% notes (Bearer)	3,104	101. 0. 0.xd	3,030.
£ 3,000	Royal Mail Steam Packet Co. Ltd. Ordinary	2,832	92.10. 0.	2,775.
£ 2,000	Anglo Ceylon & General Estates Co. Ltd.	5,391	2.10. 0.	5,000.
1,500	Sendayan (F.M.S.) Rubber Co. Ltd. New	2,981	1.18.10.5.	2,916.
1,000	United Sua Betong Rubber Estates Ltd	2,840	2.17. 9.75.	2,890.
£ 4,000	India Rubber Gutta Percha & Telegraph Works Co. Ltd. Ordinary	3,105	1. 0. 0.	4,000.
300	Allied Chemical & Dye Corp. Shares	5,244.90	5/8=27,187.50)	5,592.
600	American Smelting & Refining Co. Shares	11,879.103	5/8=62,175.00)	12,790.
200	Eastman Kodak Co. Common Shares	4,642.106	3/4=21,350 0	4,392.
1,000	Shell Union oil Corp. Common Shares	5,122.24	1/8=24,125.00)	4,963.

The Independent Investment Company Limited Valuation of Investments on 30th June 1925 (*continued*)

		Value at or Under Cost	Middle Prices 30/6/25	Present Value
1,000	Kenneccott Copper Co. Common Shares	11,398.50	5/8=50,625.00)	10,414.
			$185,462.50	
		350,149		£ 363,514
Less deduction on a/c accrued dividends 1924/5		1,000		
Note. Dollar Exchange Taken @ 4.86.125.		£349,149		

Note: This valuation statement represents stocks denominated in the old system of pounds, shillings and pence. Great Britain didn't decimalize its currency system until 1971. Keep in mind that this portfolio was only a snapshot of a point in time. Keynes was constantly adding to the holdings and it would've looked much different in 1930 in the wake of the crash. This just provides a glimpse of what he held. Much more research is needed to examine the holding periods of each security, buy/sell prices and total returns that include dividend payments.

Endnotes

Foreword

1. John Maynard Keynes, *Review of Common Stocks as Long Term Investments* (Edgar Lawrence Smith, 1925).

Introduction

1. Bertrand Russell, *The Autobiography of Bertrand Russell* (Boston: Little, Brown, 1967).
2. Robert Skidelsky, *Keynes: A Very Short Introduction* (Oxford, U.K.: Oxford University Press, 2010).
3. John Maynard Keynes, *Two Memoirs: Dr. Melchior, a Defeated Enemy, and My Early Beliefs* (New York: A.M. Kelley, 1949), p. ??.
4. Ibid., p. 99.
5. Paul Krugman, introduction to *The General Theory of Employment, Interest and Money*, by John Maynard Keynes (1936; repr. New York: Palgrave Macmillan, 2007).
6. Barton Biggs, *Hedgehogging* (Hoboken, NJ: Wiley, 2006).

Chapter 1

1. Robert Skidelsky, *John Maynard Keynes, 1883-1946: Economist, Philosopher, Statesman* (New York: Penguin, 2005), pp. 105–111.
2. Robert Skidelsky, e-mail response, January 9, 2013.
3. J. M. Keynes, *A Treatise on Probability* (1921; repr. Hong Kong: Forgotten Books, 2012), p. 52.

4. John Kay, "The Other Multiplier Effect," *Financial Times*, August 4, 2012.
5. J. M. Keynes, 1910 Lenten Term lecture notes, King's College archives.
6. Ibid.
7. Roy Harrod, *The Life of John Maynard Keynes* (New York: Harcourt Brace, 1951), p. 163.
8. Skidelsky, *John Maynard Keynes*, pp. 180–185.
9. Ibid., p. 249.
10. J. M. Keynes, *The Economic Consequences of the Peace* (London: Macmillan, 1919), p. 257.
11. Ibid., p. 297.

Chapter 2

1. Adam Smith, *The Theory of Moral Sentiments* (Kapaau, Hawaii: 1790; repr. Guttenberg, 2011).
2. Roy Harrod, *The Life of John Maynard Keynes* (New York: Harcourt Brace, 1951), p. 286.
3. http://virus.stanford.edu/uda/.
4. Robert Skidelsky, e-mail response, January 9, 2013.
5. Liaquat Ahamed, *The Lords of Finance: The Bankers Who Broke the World* (New York: Penguin, 2009), p. 165.
6. Ibid.
7. Donald Moggridge, *Maynard Keynes: An Economist's Biography* (London: Routledge, 1992), p. 351.
8. *Collected Writings of John Maynard Keynes*, ed. Donald Moggridge, vol. 12, (London: Macmillan, 1971–1989), pp. 4–11.
9. John Maynard Keynes, *A Tract on Monetary Reform* (1924; repr. Amherst, NY: Prometheus, 2000).
10. Ibid., p. 3.
11. Ibid., p. 2.
12. Ibid., pp. 30–31.
13. Investopedia, http://www.investopedia.com/terms/q/quantity_theory _of_money.asp#axzz2KPwxKW1r.
14. Keynes, *Tract*, p. 80.
15. National Bureau of Economic Research, http://www.nber.org/cycles /recessions_faq.html.
16. Keynes, *Tract*, pp. 175–176.

17. Milton Friedman, "John Maynard Keynes," *Economic Quarterly*, Federal Reserve Bank of Richmond, 1997, http://www.richmondfed .org/publications/research/economic_quarterly/1997/spring/pdf /friedman.pdf.
18. Keynes, *Collected Writings*, vol. 12, p. 255.
19. Investopedia, http://www.investopedia.com/terms/c/calloption .asp#axzz2KPwxKW1r.
20. Keynes, *Collected Writings*, vol. 12, pp. 260–261.
21. Ibid., p. 265.
22. Ibid., p. 32.
23. Maria Cristina Marcuzzo, ed., *Speculation and Regulation in Commodity Markets: The Keynesian Approach in Theory and Practice*, 2012, pp. vi to ix. Dipartimento di Scienze Statistiche–Sapienza Università di Roma, November 2012.
24. Ibid., p. xi.
25. Ibid., p. 8.
26. Ibid., p. 15.
27. Ibid., p. 43.
28. Ibid., p. 111.
29. Robert Skidelsky, *Keynes: The Return of the Master* (New York: Public Affairs, 2009).
30. CW, vol. 12, p. 647.
31. Morningstar.com, http://performance.morningstar.com/funds/etf /total-returns.action?t=DBC&region=USA&culture=en-us.

Chapter 3

1. John Kenneth Galbraith, *The Great Crash: 1929* (Boston: Houghton Mifflin, 1954, 1979), p. 137.
2. Polly Hill and Richard Keynes (eds.), *Lydia and Maynard: The Letters of John Maynard Keynes and Lydia Lopokova* (New York: Scribner's, 1989), p. 17.
3. Robert Skidelsky, *John Maynard Keynes: Economist, Philosopher, Statesman* (New York: Penguin, 2003), p. 416.
4. Ibid., p. 418.
5. Donald Moggridge, *Maynard Keynes: An Economist's Biography* (London: Routledge, 1992), p. 409.
6. Ibid., p. 410.

7. *Collected Writings of John Maynard Keynes*, ed. Donald Moggridge, vol. 12 (London: Macmillan, 1971–1989), p. 31; King's College Archives.

8. John Maynard Keynes, *A Treatise on Money*, vol. 1 (1930; repr. London: Martino, 2011), p. 53.

9. Ibid., p. 172.

10. Ibid., p. 293.

11. Ibid., vol. 2, p. 149.

12. Ibid., p. 197.

13. Charles Kindleberger, *Manias, Panics and Crashes: A History of Financial Crises* (New York: Basic Books, 1989), pp. 25–26.

14. Ibid., p. 151.

15. Keynes, *Collected Writings*, vol. 12, p. 31.

16. Statement from P.R. Finance Co., 1935, King's College archives, JMK/PR/2.

17. Ibid., 1935.

18. Ibid., 1934 (annual meeting speech to shareholders).

19. Ibid., 1933.

20. Ibid., 1933.

21. Ibid., 1932.

22. Ibid., 1931.

23. Ibid., 1930.

24. Ibid., 1929.

25. Gavyn Davies, "Keynes the Hedge Fund Pioneer," *Financial Times*, August 22, 2012, www.ft.com.

26. Keynes, "1931 memo to National Mutual Life Insurance Company," *Collected Writings*, vol. 12, as quoted in Barton Biggs, *Hedgehogging* (Hoboken, NJ: Wiley, 2006).

27. Ibid.

Chapter 4

1. William Silber, *Volcker: The Triumph of Persistence* (New York: Bloomsbury, 2012), p. 35.

2. Sylvia Nasar, *Grand Pursuit: The Story of Economic Genius* (New York: Simon & Schuster, 2011), p. 307.

3. Ibid., p. 310.

4. Ibid., p. 311.

5. William Bernstein, *Skating Where the Puck Was: The Correlation Game in a Flat World* (Investing for Adults, eBook II) (Bernstein, 2012), p. 5.
6. Ibid.
7. Jess Chua and Richard Woodward, "J. M. Keynes's Investment Performance: A Note," *Journal of Finance*, March 1983, p. 233.
8. *Ibbotson SBBI 2012 Classic Yearbook* (Chicago: Morningstar, 2012), p. 33.
9. David Chambers, Elroy Dimson and J. Foo "Keynes the Stock Market Investor: The Inception of Institutional Equity Investing," *Journal of Financial and Quantitative Analysis*, 2013 (in press) and Chambers, D. and Dimson, E., "John Maynard Keynes the Investment Innovator," *Journal of Economic Perspectives*, Vol 27, Number 3, Summer, 2013, pp. 1–18.
10. Ibid., p. 3.
11. Ibid.
12. Ibid., p. 8.
13. *Journal of Financial and Quantitative Analysis*, 2013.
14. Chambers, Dimson, and Foo, "Keynes the Stock Market Investor: The Inception of Institutional Equity Investing,"pp. 1–18.
15. John Maynard Keynes the Investment Innovator.
16. Keynes the stock market innovator.
17. Ibid., p. 13.
18. Ibid.
19. Chambers, Dimson, and Foo, "Keynes the Stock Market Investor: The Inception of Institutional Equity Investing,"pp. 2–3.
20. Ibid.
21. Letter to Richard Kahn, May 1938, in *Collected Writings of John Maynard Keynes*, ed. Donald Moggridge, vol. 12 (London: Macmillan, 1971–1989), p. 100.
22. Chambers and Dimson, *Keynes*, p. 29.
23. See Daniel Kahneman, *Thinking, Fast and Slow* (New York: Farrar, Straus and Giroux, 2011), for an extensive explanation of behavioral economics and prospect theory.

Chapter 5

1. Peter Clarke, *Keynes: The Rise, Fall and Return of the 20th Century's Most Influential Economist* (New York: Bloomsbury Press, 2009), p. 51.
2. IMDb, http://www.imdb.com/title/tt0034240/?ref_=fn_al_tt_1.
3. John F. Wasik, *The Merchant of Power: Sam Insull, Thomas Edison, and the Creation of the Modern Metropolis* (New York: Palgrave Macmillan, 2006).
4. Clarke, *Keynes*, p. 76.
5. John Maynard Keynes, *The General Theory of Employment, Interest and Money* (1936; repr. Cambridge, UK: Macmillan/BN Publishing, 2008), p. 7.
6. Benjamin Graham, *The Intelligent Investor* (1950; repr. New York: Harper & Row, 1973).
7. George Akerlof and Robert Shiller, *Animal Spirits: How Human Psychology Drives the Economy, and Why It Matters for Global Capitalism* (Princeton, NJ: Princeton University Press, 2009), p. 14.
8. Ibid.
9. John Kenneth Galbraith, *Economics in Perspective* (Boston: Houghton Mifflin, 1987), p. 233.
10. Paul Krugman, introduction to *The General Theory of Employment, Interest and Money*, by John Maynard Keynes (New York: Palgrave Macmillan, 2007), p. 8.
11. Ibid., p. 7.
12. Ibid., p. 1.
13. http://usgovinfo.about.com/od/thepresidentandcabinet/a/did-bush-say-go-shopping-after-911.htm.
14. Keynes, *General Theory*, p. 98.
15. Investopedia, http://www.investopedia.com/terms/b/bookvalue.asp#axzz2LHsGutnX.
16. Keynes, *General Theory*, p. 99.
17. Ibid., p. 101.
18. Ibid.
19. Ibid.
20. Ibid., p. 102.
21. Ibid., p. 101.
22. Ibid., p. 103.

23. Ibid., p. 104.
24. Ibid.
25. Ibid.
26. Ibid., p. 106.
27. Ibid., p. 247.
28. Donald Moggridge, ed., *Keynes on the Wireless* (New York: Palgrave Macmillan, 2010), p. 57, from a radio show on January 14, 1931.
29. Peter Clarke, *The Keynesian Revolution in the Making, 1924–1936* (Oxford, UK: Clarendon, 1988), p. 288.
30. Roger Backhouse and Bradley Bateman, *Capitalist Revolutionary: John Maynard Keynes* (Cambridge, MA: Harvard University Press, 2011), p. 93.
31. Hyman Minsky, *John Maynard Keynes: Hyman P. Minsky's Influential Re-intepretation of the Keynesian Revolution* (New York: McGraw-Hill, 2008), p. 9.

Chapter 6

1. David Swensen, *Unconventional Success: A Fundamental Approach to Personal Investment* (New York: Free Press, 2005).
2. Robert Skidelsky, *John Maynard Keynes, 1883-1946: Economist, Philosopher, Statesman* (New York: Penguin, 2005), p. 565.
3. Ibid.
4. Martin Conrad, "The Money Paradox," Barrons.com, December 31, 2011.
5. John Maynard Keynes, "The Originating Causes of World Unemployment," lecture at the University of Chicago/Harris Foundation, in Quincy Wright, John Maynard Keynes, Karl Přibram, E. J. Phelan, and Norman Wait, *Unemployment as a World-Problem* (Chicago: University of Chicago Press, 1931), p. 35.
6. Ibid., p. 36.
7. Marcello De Cecco, "Keynes and Modern International Finance Theory," in *Alfred Marshall e John M. Keynes, rottura o continuita*, ed. Mauro Ridolfi (Maggioli Editore, 1980).
8. Ibid., p. 239.
9. Ibid., p. 239.
10. Akerlof web page, University of California–Berkeley, https://www .econ.berkeley.edu/faculty/803.

11. "Book Review: *Animal Spirits* by Akerlof and Shiller," *Financial Times*, February 17, 2009.
12. George Akerlof and Robert Shiller, *Animal Spirits: How Human Psychology Drives the Economy, and Why It Matters for Global Capitalism* (Princeton, NJ: Princeton University Press, 2009), p. 4.
13. Ibid.
14. Ibid., p. 5.
15. Ibid., p. 17.
16. Ibid., p. 29.
17. Ibid., p. 42.
18. Ibid., p. 131.
19. Ibid., p. 136.
20. Telephone interview with Robert Shiller at Yale, January 17, 2013.
21. Akerlof and Shiller, *Animal Spirits*, p. 146.
22. Hersh Shefrin and Meir Statman, "Behavioral Finance in the Financial Crisis: Market Efficiency, Minsky, and Keynes," Santa Clara (CA) University, November 2011, p. 3.
23. Ibid.
24. Lee Munson, *Rigged Money: Beating Wall Street at Its Own Game* (Hoboken, NJ: Wiley, 2012), p. 161.
25. Brad Barber and Terrence Odean, "The Courage of Misguided Convictions: The Trading Behavior of Individual Investors," SSRN, April 12, 2000.
26. Daniel Kahneman, *Thinking, Fast and Slow* (New York: Farrar, Straus and Giroux, 2011).
27. Daniel Kahneman, personal interview, January 10, 2012.
28. John Maynard Keynes, "How to Avoid a Slump," *Times London Independent Conservative Daily* (London)/The Living Age, March 1937, p. 13.

Chapter 7

1. John Maynard Keynes, Home Service broadcast, September 23, 1940, in Donald Moggridge, ed., *Keynes on the Wireless* (New York: Palgrave Macmillan, 2010), pp. 204–205; republished in *The Listener*, 436;455, xxii, 240–5.
2. Robert Skidelsky, *John Maynard Keynes, 1883-1946: Economist, Philosopher, Statesman* (New York: Penguin, 2005), pp. 580–582.

3. Ibid., p. 583.
4. E-mail from Robert Skidelsky, January 9, 2013.
5. Barton Biggs, *Hedgehogging* (Hoboken, NJ: Wiley, 2006), p. 301.
6. Ibid. Inflation adjustment mine, using the Bureau of Labor Statistics inflation calculator.
7. This is an incredibly conservative estimate. Keynes donated many of his paintings and books to museums, and they would have been worth considerably more on the open market.
8. Biggs, *Hedgehogging*, p. 301.
9. *Collected Writings of John Maynard Keynes*, ed. Donald Moggridge, vol. 12 (London: Macmillan, 1971–1989), quoted in Charles Ellis and James Vertin, *Classics: An Investor's Anthology* (Homewood, IL: Dow Jones-Irwin, 1989), p. 77.
10. Ibid., pp. 77–78.
11. Ibid., p. 78.
12. Ibid., p. 79.
13. Ibid., p. 80.
14. Ibid.
15. Ibid.
16. Ibid., p. 84.
17. Ibid.
18. Ibid.
19. Ibid., p. 85.
20. Gavyn Davies, "Keynes the Hedge Fund Pioneer," *Financial Times*, August 22, 2012.
21. Oliver Westall, *The Provincial Insurance Company 1903–38: Family, Markets and Competitive Growth* (Manchester, U.K.: Manchester University Press, 1992), p. 369.
22. John Maynard Keynes, Letter to F. C. Scott, in Westall, *Provincial*, p. 369.
23. Westall, *Provincial*, p. 380.
24. Ibid., p. 365.
25. Keynes, *Collected Writings*, vol. 12, p. 11.
26. Ibid.
27. Ibid., p. 81.
28. Ibid., p. 83.

Chapter 8

1. Robert Skidelsky, *J. M. Keynes 1883–1946: Economist, Philosopher, Statesman* (New York: Penguin, 2005), p. 617.
2. Donald Moggridge, *Maynard Keynes: An Economist's Biography* (London: Routledge, 1992), p. 641.
3. Ibid.
4. Ibid.
5. Charles Ellis, *Classics: An Investor's Anthology* (Homewood, IL: Dow Jones-Irwin, 1989), p. 85.
6. Benjamin Graham, *The Intelligent Investor*, 4th ed. (New York: Harper & Row, 1973), p. 109.
7. Ibid., p. 279.
8. As quoted in Alice Schroeder, *The Snowball: Warren Buffett and the Business of Life* (New York: Bantam Dell, 2008), p. 21.
9. Ibid., p. 20.
10. Roger Lowenstein, *Buffett: The Making of an American Capitalist* (New York: Random House, 1995), p. 103.
11. Ibid.
12. Mary Buffett and David Clark, *The Warren Buffett Stock Portfolio: Warren Buffett's Stock Picks: Why and When He Is Investing in Them* (New York: Scribner, 2011).
13. Ibid.
14. Andrea Frazzini, David Kabiller, and Lasse Pedersen, "Buffett's Alpha," Yale University Department of Economics, August 29, 2012, http://www.econ.yale.edu/~af227/pdf/Buffett%27s%20Alpha%20-%20Frazzini,%20Kabiller%20and%20Pedersen.pdf, p. 1.
15. E-mail response to author query sent to Warren Buffett (reply by Ms. Bosanek), 10/11/12.
16. Robert Hagstrom, *The Warren Buffett Portfolio: Mastering the Power of the Focus Investment Strategy* (New York: Wiley, 1989), p. 41.
17. E-mail reply from Alice Schroeder, author of *Snowball*, January 10, 2013.
18. E-mail reply from Debbie Bosanek, assistant to Warren Buffett, October 11, 2012. My request for an interview with Buffett was denied.

19. David Swensen, *Pioneering Portfolio Management* (New York: Free Press, 2009), p. 2.
20. Ibid.
21. Ibid., p. 64.
22. Ibid.
23. Ibid., p. 69.
24. Ibid., p. 89.
25. *Baseball Almanac*, http://www.baseball-almanac.com/players/player.php?p=keelewi01.
26. Swensen, *Pioneering*, p. 92.
27. Ibid., p. 107.
28. Ibid.
29. Personal interview with Daniel Kahneman, January 10, 2012.
30. Ibid.
31. Jeremy Grantham, "Welcome to Dystopia! Entering a Long-Term and Politically Dangerous Food Crisis," *GMO Quarterly Letter*, July 2012, https://www.gmo.com/America/_AdminPages/_Search.htm.
32. Ibid., p. 4.
33. Daniel Kadlec, "Index Funds Win Again, This Time by a Landslide," *Time*, February 24, 2012.
34. John Bogle, interview, November 20, 2012.
35. "The (Non) Lesson of History—and the (Real) Lessons of Return Sources and Investment Costs," speech by John Bogle before the American Philosophical Society, Philadelphia, November 10, 2012.
36. Ibid., p. 3.
37. Ibid., p. 4.
38. Ibid., p. 5.
39. Ibid.

Chapter 9

1. Joseph Stiglitz, *The Price of Inequality* (New York: Norton, 2012), p. 105.
2. Donald Moggridge, *Maynard Keynes: An Economist's Biography* (London: Routledge, 1992), pp. 834–835.
3. Ibid., p. 835.
4. Ibid., p. 836.

5. "Lord Keynes Dies of Heart Attack," *Times* (London), quoted in Robert Skidelsky, *John Maynard Keynes, 1883–1946: Economist, Philosopher, Statesman* (New York: Penguin, 2005), p. 833.

6. Ibid.

7. Ibid., p. 834.

8. Ibid., p. 836.

9. The Leuthold Group, *Inside the Stock Market*, monthly newsletter, March 2013, pp. 5–6.

10. *Ibbotson SBBI Classic Yearbook* (Chicago: Morningstar, 2012), p. 32.

11. Ibid.

12. Ibid., p. 32.

13. Ibid.

14. Dan Kadlec, "Index Funds Win Again—This Time by a Landslide," *Time*, February 24, 2012, http://business.time.com/2012/02/24/index-funds-win-again-this-time-by-a-landslide/.

15. Ibid.

16. Ibbotson SBBI 2013 Classic Yearbook: Market Results for Stocks, Bonds, Bills and Inflation 1926–2012 (Morningstar, 2013)," pp. 37-43.

17. Andre Malabre Jr., *Lost Prophets: An Insider's History of the Modern Economists* (Boston: Harvard Business Review Press, 1994), p. 27.

18. John Maynard Keynes, "How to Avoid a Slump," *Times* (London), March 1937.

19. John Maynard Keynes, *The End of Laissez-Faire* (London: BN Publishing, 1924).

20. Ibid., p. 41.

21. Ibid.

22. John Kenneth Galbraith, *The Great Crash, 1929* (Boston: Houghton Mifflin, 1979), p. 177.

23. John Maynard Keynes, "Economic Possibilities for Our Grandchildren," in *Essays in Persuasion* (1930; repr. New York: Norton, 1963), p. 368.

24. Ibid.

25. Robert Skidelsky and Edward Skidelsky, *How Much Is Enough? Money and the Good Life* (New York: Other Press, 2012), p. 20.

26. Ibid., p. 218.

Epilogue

1. Robert Skidelsky, *Keynes: A Very Short Introduction* (Oxford, U.K.: Oxford University Press, 2010), p. 169.
2. Brief meeting with Paul Krugman after Chicago lecture at the Chicago Council of Global Affairs, January 28, 2013.
3. Paul Krugman, "Hawks and Hypocrites," *New York Times*, November 12, 2012.
4. Paul Krugman, *End This Depression Now!* (New York: Norton, 2012), p. 237.
5. Joseph Stiglitz, *The Price of Inequality: How Today's Divided Society Endangers Our Future* (New York: Norton, 2012), p. 267.
6. Robert Skidelsky, *Keynes: The Return of the Master* (New York: Public Affairs, 2009), p. 116.
7. Thomas Geoghegan, "What Would Keynes Do?" *Nation*, October 17, 2011, p. 15.
8. Vince Cable, "Keynes Would Be on Our Side," *New Statesman*, January 17, 2011, p. 33.
9. Robert Kuttner, "Economic Recovery and Social Investment: A Strategy to Create Good Jobs in the Service Sector," New America Foundation, 2012.
10. Alan Bjerga, *Endless Appetites: How the Commodities Casino Creates Hunger and Unrest* (Hoboken, NJ: Bloomberg Press, 2011), p. 58.
11. Al Gore, speech, Chicago Council on Global Affairs, Chicago, February 8, 2013.
12. John Kenneth Galbraith, *The Affluent Society* (Boston: Houghton Mifflin, 1976), p. 270.

Appendix B

1. *Collected Writings of John Maynard Keynes*, ed. Donald Moggridge, vol. 12 (London: Macmillan, 1971–1989), p. 34.
2. Ibid.
3. "The People History, 1925," http://www.thepeoplehistory.com/1925.html.
4. Keynes, *Collected Writings*, vol. 12, p. 36.

Bibliographical Notes

Backhouse, Roger, and Bradley Bateman. *The Cambridge Companion to Keynes*. Cambridge, U.K.: Cambridge University Press, 2006. An insightful collection of essays covering the many aspects of Keynes's career.

———. *Capitalist Revolutionary: John Maynard Keynes*. Cambridge, MA: Harvard University Press, 2011. The authors examine the impact of the Keynesian revolution.

Bell, Quentin. *Bloomsbury Recalled*. New York: Columbia University Press, 1995. Bell brings the Bloomsbury group alive in this short series of profiles, one of which is on Keynes.

Bogle, John C. *The Battle for the Soul of Capitalism*. New Haven, CT: Yale University Press, 2005. An essential read from the mutual fund giant.

Clarke, Peter. *Keynes: The Rise, Fall, and Return of the 20th Century's Most Influential Economist*, New York: Bloomsbury Press, 2009. Clarke, a historian, places Keynes in a modern perspective.

———. *The Keynesian Revolution in the Making: 1924–1936* (Oxford, U.K.: Clarendon Press, 1988). Clarke details the evolution of Keynes's economic thought.

Galbraith, John Kenneth. The great Harvard economist, Kennedy and Johnson administration stalwart, and former ambassador provides a useful lens for Keynes in his many works, most notably:

———. *The Great Crash, 1929*. Boston: Houghton Mifflin, 1954/1979.

———. *Money: Whence It Came, Where It Went*. Boston: Houghton Mifflin, 1975.

———. *The Affluent Society*, 3rd ed. Boston: Houghton Mifflin, 1976.

Harrod, Roy. *The Life of John Maynard Keynes*. New York: Easton Press/ Harcourt, Brace, 1951/1990. As a disciple of Keynes, Harrod was intimately connected to Keynes in his later years. While this is a good first book to read on Keynes, Harrod is far too close to his subject to give an objective evaluation of Keynes's work.

Hill, Polly, and Richard Keynes, eds. *Lydia and Maynard: The Letters of John Maynard Keynes and Lydia Lopokova*. New York: Scribners, 1989. This charming collection of letters between Keynes and his future wife present more of the economist's personal side.

Collected Writings of John Maynard Keynes. London: Macmillan, 1971– 1989. Edited by Donald Moggridge, the managing editor of the series. The full collection was published for the Royal Economic Society by Macmillan. I relied most heavily upon Volume 12, *Economic Articles and Correspondence: Investment and Editorial*, which summarizes most of Keynes's investment activities and contains many of his letters regarding his portfolio management methods.

Keynes, John Maynard. You have to read Keynes's own prose to appreciate the depth of his intellectual ocean. While the *General Theory* and the *Treatise on Probability* are probably his most difficult works—best suited for those with backgrounds in economics and statistics—his essays and *Economic Consequences* run the gamut from didactic to utopian.

_____. *The Economic Consequences of the Peace*. London: Macmillan, 1919. A must-read for all history students and policy makers, this powerful indictment of the Versailles Treaty spells out how nations can survive after a war. It influenced the Marshall Plan and most postwar thinking about how victors can avoid future wars. This edition also includes his criticism of free-market economics, *The End of Laissez-Faire*, 1924.

_____. *Essays in Biography*, New York: Harcourt, Brace, 1933. Keynes's short takes on people he admired, including Churchill, Malthus, and Alfred Marshall, his mentor.

_____. *Essays in Persuasion*. New York: Norton, 1963. This highly readable collection contains his seminal "Economic Possibilities for Our Grandchildren," an optimistic piece written in 1930.

_____. *The General Theory of Employment, Interest and Money*. 1936. Reprinted with an introduction by Paul Krugman. New York: Palgrave Macmillan, 2007. Keynes's masterpiece, which introduced "animal spirits" and "beauty contest" into investment parlance, is put into modern perspective by Nobel Prize winner Krugman.

———. *A Tract on Monetary Reform*. 1924. Reprinted Amherst, NY: Prometheus, 2000. This short, early volume contains some key insights on inflation and savings.

———. *A Treatise on Money*. 1930. Reprinted London: Martino, 2011. Written at the beginning of the Great Depression, this two-volume compendium is an often-compelling read on the history of money, monetary policy, savings, investment, and commodity pricing.

———. *A Treatise on Probability*. 1921. Reprinted Hong Kong: Forgotten Books, 2012. Regarded as Keynes's first major academic work, this book lays the groundwork for some of his views on investment management.

King's College Archives, University of Cambridge, Cambridge, U.K. Ensconced in a well-catalogued collection are nearly all of Keynes's papers, including records of his investment activities. Archivist Patricia McGuire has done an excellent job of organizing the Keynes materials, which I searched with permission.

Krugman, Paul. *End This Depression Now!* New York: Norton, 2012. Although his focus is on economic malaise (as of 2013), Krugman advocates Keynesian approaches.

———. *The Return of Depression Economics and the Crisis of 2008*. New York: Norton, 2009. Krugman's neo-Keynesian analysis of the great meltdown.

Moggridge, Donald. *Maynard Keynes: An Economist's Biography*. London: Routledge, 1992. As the managing editor of Keynes's collected works (see above) Moggridge has some important insights into Keynes's investment work, although he's not as complete as Skidelsky.

———, ed. *Keynes on the Wireless*. New York: Palgrave Macmillan, 2010. This collection of transcripts of some of Keynes's key radio broadcasts shows the economist as a multimedia personality.

Minsky, Hyman. *John Maynard Keynes: Hyman Minsky's Influential Re-Interpretation of the Keynesian Revolution*. New York: McGraw-Hill, 2008. A leading interpreter of Keynes's theories provides some modern insights.

Nasar, Sylvia. *Grand Pursuit: The Story of Economic Genius*. New York: Simon & Schuster, 2011. The author of the acclaimed *A Beautiful*

Mind provides a flowing narrative on the evolution of modern economics and features Keynes and his contemporaries in several sections.

Scrase, David, and Peter Croft. *Maynard Keynes: Collector of Pictures, Books
and Manuscripts*. Cambridge, U.K.: King's College, 1983. This edited
catalogue of Keynes's art and manuscript collection details some of the
great artwork and books that he owned.

Skidelsky, Robert. Skidelsky's contribution to our understanding of Keynes
is immeasurable. He is to Keynes what Manchester was to Churchill
and Caro is to Lyndon Baines Johnson. He's essential reading for a full
picture of the man and his work, mainly through his three-volume
biography. I relied heavily upon Skidelsky's condensed biography, *John
Maynard Keynes, 1883–1946: Economist, Philosopher, Statesman*. He
also revisited Keynes after the 2008 crash (*The Return of the Master*)
and examined Keynes's views on prosperity in *How Much Is Enough?*

———. *John Maynard Keynes, 1883–1946: Economist, Philosopher,
Statesman*. New York: Penguin, 2005.

———. *John Maynard Keynes: A Biography*. Vol. 1, *Hopes Betrayed
1883–1920*. New York: Penguin, 1994.

———. *John Maynard Keynes*. Vol. 2, *The Economist as Savior
1920–1937*. New York: Penguin, 1995.

———. *John Maynard Keynes*. Vol. 3, *Fighting for Britain 1937–1946*.
London: Penguin, 2001.

———. *Keynes: A Very Short Introduction*. Oxford, U.K.: Oxford
University Press, 2010.

———. *Keynes: The Return of the Master*. New York: Public Affairs, 2009.

———. and Edward Skidelsky. *How Much Is Enough? Money and the Good
Life*. New York: Other Press, 2012.

Stiglitz, Joseph. *The Price of Inequality: How Today's Divided Society
Endangers Our Future*. New York: Norton, 2012. Although not
focused exclusively on Keynes, the Nobel Prize–winning economist,
a neo-Keynesian, examines many of the economic disparities that
Keynes warned about.

Wapshott, Nicholas. *Keynes Hayek: The Clash That Defined Modern
Economics*. New York: Norton, 2011. The often-entertaining account
of the rivalry between the two economists and what it means for
today's debate on economic policy.

Westall, Oliver. *The Provincial Insurance Company 1903–38: Family, Markets and Competitive Growth*, Manchester, U.K.: Manchester University Press, 1992. A brief history of the British insurance company with a focus on Keynes's role as investment manager.

Index

A.D. Investment Trust Ltd., 27–28, 38
  and P.R. Finance Company, 40
The Affluent Society (Galbraith), 156
Ahamed, Liaquat, 17
Akerlof, George, 92–93, 94, 96
alternative investments, 128
anchoring, 100
animal spirits, 4, 78, 80, 83, 85
  as the beginning of behavioral economics, 92–97
  how they take shape as an economic catalyst, 96–97
  and market inefficiency, 97–101
  role of, 94–96, 139
  spurning, 102–103
Animal Spirits (Akerlof and Shiller), 93
art collection, 157–158, 159
austerity, 152–153
austerity economics, 152
automatic economic resets, 76

Backhouse, Roger, 85
backwardation
  defined, 24
  normal backwardation, 29, 58
Balanchine, George, 36
Barber, Brad, 99–100
Bateman, Bradley, 85

behavioral economics, 67, 131–132
  See also animal spirits
behavioral factors influencing commodity prices, 25–26
believability, 4
Bell, Clive, 45
Bell, Vanessa, 19, 158
Bernstein, William, 57
Biggs, Barton, 107–108
Blackett, Basil, 19
Bogle, John C. "Jack", 133–136
bonds, vs. stocks, 139–140
book value, 80–81
Bosanek, Debbie, 128
Brainard, William, 130
Bretton Woods system, 124, 146–147, 153
Brown, W. Langdon, 19
Buffett (Lowenstein), 126–127
Buffett, Warren, 68, 76, 116, 125–128
Bush, George W., 79–80
buy low and hold, 80

Cable, Vincent, 154
call options, defined, 24
Cambridge (city), 157, 158–159
Cambridge University, Keynes returning to, 2
CAPE, 101–102

capitalism, 72, 97
Cassel, Ernest (Sir), 19
certainty, 140
Chambers, David, 62
Chest Fund, 59–61
China, economic growth of, 153–154
Chua, Jess, 59, 61, 62
Churchill, Winston, 53–54
civil service career, 1–2
commodities, 24–27
    A.D. Investment Trust Ltd.,
      27–28
    behavioral factors influencing
      commodity prices, 25–26
    collapse in demand, 31–32
    and correlation risk, 57
    cotton, 30
    Keynes's trading performance,
      28–31
    prices, 58–59
    tin, 30
    wheat, 30–31
    why commodities are still
      dangerous, 32–33
commodity inflation, 41
*Common Stocks as Long-Term
    Investments* (Smith), 63–64, 126
Conference Board reports, 95
confidence, 43–44, 89–90, 94–95
    in a company's forecast, 80
    and employment, 77
    irrational elements affecting, 78
    and marginal propensity to
      consume, 78
    overconfidence bias, 99–100
Conrad, Martin, 88–89
contango, 58
    defined, 25
contrarian investing, 130, 142
Cooke, Russell, 37
correlation, 55–56
    commodities and correlation
      risk, 57
    inverse correlation, 141

corruption, 95
cost matters hypothesis, 135–136
credit cycles, 37–39
    See also cycles
credit-cycling, 67
currency markets, 13
    Keynes's speculation in, 17–20
Curzon, F.N., 90, 109–110
cycles
    how Keynes tracked, 40–42
    See also credit cycles
cyclically adjusted price-earnings
    ratio. *See* CAPE

Davies, Gavyn, 115–116
De Cecco, Marcello, 92
death of Keynes, 138
deception of average investors,
    95–96
defensive stocks, 121
demand, lack of demand leading
    to unemployment, 76–77
Dimson, Elroy, 62
diversification, 38–39, 136, 141
    See also opposed risks
dividend growth, 52
dividend income, 64
dividend payers, 51–52
dividends, 141–142
Dolin, Anton, 36
dollar cost averaging, 6, 13, 121
dominant narrative, 96–97

earning power, 125, 127
Economic Consequences of the Peace
    (Keynes), 11–13
Economic Journal, 9
Economics in Perspective (Galbraith),
    79
enterprise, 135
enterprise value, 129–130
erosion of living standards,
    152–153
Estates Committee, 9

evils of speculation
   Keynes's definition, 8
   See also speculation
excessive optimism, 100

fairness, 95
faithfulness, 106
   See also pet stocks
Falk, Oswald, 7, 16
   and A.D. Investment Trust Ltd.,
     38
   clashes with Keynes, 45, 91, 106
   Independent Investment
     Company, 161, 162
   investments before the stock
     market crash, 35
   in Keynes's investing syndicate, 17
FDR. *See* Roosevelt, Franklin Delano
Fisher, Irving, 22, 32, 95–96
flexibility, 115
   and gumption, 145–146
focus approach, 65
Fonteyn, Margot, 138
framing errors, 100
Frazzini, Andrea, 127
Friedman, Milton, 24
future investment needed, 154–156

Galbraith, John Kenneth, 78–79,
   147, 156
gambling, 7
   Keynes's definition, 8
General Theory of Employment,
   Interest and Money (Keynes),
   4, 74–75
   insights for investors, 80–84
   what it means to investors, 75–80
Geoghegan, Thomas, 154
George, David Lloyd, 53
gold standard, 20, 22, 23, 72
Gore, Al, 155
gradualism, 130
Graham, Benjamin, 68, 76, 116,
   125–127

Grand Pursuit (Nasar), 54–55
Grant, Duncan, 2, 19, 36, 158
Grantham, Jeremy, 132–133
Great Depression, 31–32
Greenspan, Alan, 43
gumption, and flexibility, 145–146

Hagstrom, Robert, 127–128
Hayek, Friedrich, 54, 138
health of Keynes, 84–85, 87–88
hedge funds
   A.D. Investment Trust Ltd.,
     27–28
   defined, 18
   Keynes's investing syndicate,
     17–20
Hedgehogging (Biggs), 107–108
hedging, 13
Hill, A.V., 19
Hoover, Herbert, 54
hyperinflation, 21

IIC. *See* Independent Investment
   Company
Independent Investment Company,
   portfolio, 161–167
index fund, 134, 136
Indian Currency and Finance
   (Keynes), 9
industrial index, 91, 116
inequality, 152–153
inflation
   in Germany following World
     War I, 12
   hyperinflation, 21
   impacts of, 21–22
Insull, Samuel, 72
Intelligent Investor (Graham), 76,
   125–126, 130
International Monetary Fund, 124,
   137, 152
intrinsic value, 48, 68–69, 141
   See also value investing
inverse correlation, 141

investing
  Keynes's interest in, 2–3
  portfolio prior to World War I,
    5–7
  See also value investing
investment, 41
  vs. speculation, 82–83
investment policy, 121–122, 132
  long-range, 142–143
investment policy statements,
    108–109, 121, 136
investment return, 135
irrational exuberance, 43
  See also confidence
Irrational Exuberance (Shiller), 93

Kabiller, David, 127
Kahn, Richard, 88
Kahneman, Daniel, 67, 92, 99, 100,
    101
  and the behavioral economics
    school, 131–132
Keynes, Geoffrey, 17, 45
Keynes, Margaret, 19
Keynes, John Neville, 18–19, 45
Keynesian compact, 152
Keynesian stimulus, 54, 79–80,
    151
keys to wealth, 139–144
Kindleberger, Charles, 43–44
King's College
  holding pet stocks in portfolio,
    111–114
  Keynes's success at, 61–66
King's College Chest Fund. *See* Chest
    Fund
Krugman, Paul, 79, 89, 151–152
Kuttner, Robert, 155

leverage, 117–118, 119, 130–131
life before World War I, 9–10
long-range investment policy,
    142–143
Lopokova, Lydia, 15, 36, 85, 124

Lords of Finance (Ahamed), 17
Lost Prophets (Malabre), 147
Lowenstein, Roger, 126–127

magneto trouble, 77
Malabre, Andre, Jr., 147
Manias, Panics and Crashes
    (Kindleberger), 43
manuscript collection, 157–158, 159
Marcuzzo, Maria Cristina, 29
margin of safety, 126
  See also safety first policy
marginal propensity to consume, 78
Marine Insurance, 6
market inefficiency, and animal
    spirits, 97–101
market timing, 129
Markowitz, Harry, 55
Marshall, Alfred, 3, 72
Mather & Platt, 6
McGuire, Patricia, 158
"The Means to Prosperity" (Keynes),
    84
mean-variance optimization, 55–56
Mellon, Andrew, 54
mental accounting, 100
methods of speculation
  See also speculation
Michigan Consumer Sentiment
    Index, 95
Minsky, Hyman, 85, 98
moat, 63, 127
Modern Portfolio Theory, 55, 56
Moggridge, Donald, 5, 161, 163
  Keynes's syndicate, 19–20
monetary reform, 20–24
Money Illusion (Fisher), 96
money supply, 77
Munger, Charlie, 127
Munson, Lee, 99

Nasar, Sylvia, 54
National Bureau of Economic
    Research, 23

National Mutual Life Assurance
Society, 63, 88, 90–91
clash with board over holding pet
stocks, 106
letter to chairman outlining
Keynes's principles, 109–110
Keynes on the board of, 16
net worth, 119
New Deal, 72
Newton, Isaac, 138
normal backwardation, 58
See also backwardation

Odean, Terrance, 100
opposed risks, 27, 38–39, 55–56, 58
alternative investments, 128
balancing your portfolio, 140–141
See also diversification
optimism, excessive, 100
overconfidence bias, 99–100
overtrading, 136

paradox of thrift, 78–79
passive investment, 143
Pedersen, Lasse, 127
pet stocks, 107–108
clash with National Mutual board
over holding pet stocks, 106
Keynes's personal portfolio,
117–118
King's College portfolio,
111–114
measuring Keynes's success,
118–121
Provincial Insurance Company
portfolio, 115–117, 120
Pioneering Portfolio Management
(Swensen), 129
Political Economy Club, 2
portfolios
A.D. Investment Trust Ltd.,
27–28
Chest Fund, 60
early stock holdings, 5–7

Independent Investment
Company, 161–167
Keynes's personal portfolio,
72–73, 117–118, 144–145
King's College discretionary
portfolios, 112–114
King's College portfolio,
111–114
National Mutual Life Assurance
Society, 90–91
P.R. Finance Company, 39–40,
46, 49
Provincial Insurance Company
portfolio, 115–117, 120
the syndicate, 19–20
PowerShares DB Index Commodity
Tracking Fund (DBC), 33
P.R. Finance Company, 39–40,
44–48, 55
Price of Inequality (Stiglitz), 152
probability, 2, 140
Keynes using the financial
markets to test his theory of
probability, 3
A Treatise on Probability, 3–4
profit, 42
prospect theory, 67, 100
prospective yield, 86
prosperity, 144
Provincial Insurance Company,
63, 88
holding pet stocks in portfolio,
115–117, 120
purchasing power, 41
put options, defined, 25

quantity theory, 22

radical uncertainty, 4
real-time rebalancing, 129
rebalancing, 129
redistribution of wealth, 147
regulation, 147
Reinhart, Carmen, 153

residual claims on industrial growth, 64
Ricardo, David, 72
Rigged Money (Munson), 99
risk
    commodities and correlation risk, 57
    tail risk, 59
Robin Hood tax, 155
Rogoff, Kenneth, 153
Roosevelt, Franklin Delano, 72
    Keynes's audience with, 84
Royal Commission on Indian Currency and Finance, 2

safety first policy, 121, 125, 126
Samuelson, Paul, 75, 134
savings, 41
    and confidence, 78
scandal, 95
Schroeder, Alice, 128
Scott, F.C., 115, 125
Security Analysis (Graham and Dodd), 80
Sharpe, William, 55
Sharpe ratio, 127
Shaw, George Bernard, 72, 74, 138
Shefrin, Hersh, 98
Shiller, Robert, 92–93, 94, 96, 97
    and the behavioral economics school, 131–132
Skidelsky, Edward, tracking Keynes's forecast, 149–150
Skidelsky, Robert, 3, 11
    Keynes's gambling on currencies, 17
    on Keynes's multitasking, 107
    tracking Keynes's forecast, 149–150
Smith, Edgar Lawrence, 126
Soros, George, 3
speculation, 140
    vs. investment, 82–83
    Keynes's definition, 8
    overview, 51–52

    See also evils of speculation; methods of speculation
speculative return, 135
spot prices, 58
    defined, 25
statistics, 131
Statman, Meir, 98
Stiglitz, Joseph, 152
stock market crash, 31–32, 36–37
    Keynes's popularity following, 53–54
    what Keynes learned, 48–51
stock purchases, Keynes's personal stock purchases, 72–73
stocks, vs. bonds, 139–140
Strachey, Lytton, 45
Swensen, David, 128–131
syndicate, 17, 19–20

tactical asset allocators, 115
tail risk, 59
Thaler, Richard, 92
Thinking, Fast and Slow (Kahneman), 100, 131
Tobin, James, 130
Tobin's q, 130
Tract on Monetary Reform (Keynes), 20–21, 23–24
Treasury Inflation-Protected Securities (TIPS), 141
Treatise on Money (Keynes), 42
    and credit cycles, 37–39
Treatise on Probability (Keynes), 3–4
Tversky, Amos, 67, 92, 99

uncertainty, 106, 140
Unconventional Success (Swensen), 129
unemployment, lack of demand and, 76–77
U.S. Steel, 5

value investing, 62–63, 129–130
    See also intrinsic value

Versailles Treaty, Keynes's opposition
    to reparations from Germany,
    10–13
volatility, and short-term thinking, 82

war finances, Keynes consulting on,
    106

White, Harry Dexter, 124
Woodward, Richard, 59, 61, 62
Woolf, Virginia, 36
World Bank, 124, 137
World War I, Keynes's work during, 10
World War II, Keynes's work during,
    123–124

About the Author

John F. Wasik is an award-winning business journalist, speaker, and author of 14 books, including *The Merchant of Power* and *The Cul-de-Sac Syndrome*. He is also a contributor to Reuters, the *New York Times*, *Forbes*, and other national publications. He lives in Grayslake, Illinois, with his wife and two daughters.